GOVERNMENT AND THE ARTS

Debates over Federal Support of the Arts in America from George Washington to Jesse Helms

Alan Howard Levy

University Press of America, Inc.
Lanham • New York • Oxford

Copyright © 1997 by
University Press of America,® Inc.
4720 Boston Way
Lanham, Maryland 20706

12 Hid's Copse Rd.
Cummor Hill, Oxford OX2 9JJ

Library of Congress Cataloging-in-Publication Data

Levy, Alan Howard.
Government and the arts : debates over federal support of the arts in
America from George Washington to Jesse Helms/Alan Howard Levy.
p.   cm.
Includes bibliographical references and index.
l. Federal aid to the arts--United States. 2. Art Patronage--United
States. I. Title.
NX735.L48   1997 700'.973--dc21   96-52505 CIP

ISBN 0-7618-0674-1 (cloth: alk. ppr.)

♾™ The paper used in this publication meets the minimum
requirements of American National Standard for information
Sciences—Permanence of Paper for Printed Library Materials,
ANSI Z39.48—1984

*"If the Fine Arts cannot thrive in this country
without government jobs, let them fail."*

Congressman William McCoy, 1828

Contents

Introduction

In 1989 Senator Jesse Helms of North Carolina delivered a series of caustic pronouncements in regard to a few works of art which had received support from the Federal government through the National Endowment for the Arts. Sensing positive responses among the public, other critics chimed in with similar blasts. During the 1992 Republican Presidential primaries, journalist Pat Buchanan stepped up the attacks on the NEA. The remarks of Buchanan, Helms and others caused quite a stir at the offices of the National Endowments for the Arts and the Humanities as well as throughout major political and artistic circles. Buchanan had a strong showing in two early Republican primaries in New Hampshire and Georgia, and President George Bush responded by "accepting the resignation" of the Chairman of the NEA. While many wrote off the blasts against government support of the arts as mere Yahoo'ery, the remarks had significance irrespective of their intrinsic merit. People could not so cavalierly dismiss them, though many wished to, for the potential financial and political fallout was sizeable. Additionally, the question of the legitimacy of the Federal government's purview is a serious one. Official as well as private responses came forth in abundance here. Many Americans came to feel like patrons displeased with what they had sponsored. Politicians then came to see bashing the arts as a way to curry favor. The summary dismissals of Helms, Buchanan and other critics of government support of the arts ultimately pales before more general theoretical questions of the legitimacy of any such activism by the Federal government. The issue involves less the morality of the art in question and more the issue of whether the government should be involved in such genres.

In the United States there has indeed been a long standing ambivalence about the arts, about their role in society, and thus about the limits of legitimate government activism. This ambivalence is far more pronounced in the United States than in other Western nations. The following study analyzes the debates and thinking about this very matter. It is not a history of the government sponsorship of the arts, of what the government did and does, but rather an account of the history of discussions over those very issues.

Americans' ambivalence in regard to the significance and utility of the arts has always been strong. One key here has been that Americans have never been certain as to the nature of their culture. While problems of growing cultural ignorance exist in many nations, were one to question a German as to the significance of Goethe in German culture, a Frenchman about the importance of David in France, or an Englishman about Milton, the response would likely question one's intelligence if not one's sanity. The informed in many European nations are not so diverted as are educated Americans as to what goes into a cultural core. For questions as to the legitimacy of certain cultural figures, when posed to a literate American about Herman Melville, Thomas Eakins or Charles Ives, would be taken seriously and could readily engender sincere debates over whether such figures hold any significance at all.

Some late twentieth-century critics, hoisting certain political banners, regarded figures like Eakins, Melville, and Ives being of lesser significance than previously granted because of each's white, male, and Anglo-Saxon background. Such concerns, themselves essentially peripheral in relation to the content of the given art in question, reveal further the same ambivalence in American culture continues with respect to art. Within diatribes over race, gender, ethnicity and other such matters, the ignoring of the actual content of the art in question occurs in order to propagate certain political agendas. The "isms" which lend a vocabulary to such outlooks—feminism, post-structuralism, deconstructionism—flourish in other countries besides the United States, but in no other nation do they so eclipse more fundamental esthetic considerations. The artistic communities of such nations as Germany, France, and Great Britain have all debated new paradigms and integrated them into their discourse. Only in the United States did an either/or simplicity so plague discourse in the arts and letters. Such intellectual segregation and paradigmatic splitting can only occur in a nation in which the rootedness of the arts is problematic. Indeed the decline of standards in late twentieth-century American education grew as new concepts were not genuinely integrated. They came merely to provide an easy set of vocabulary cushions upon which disciples justified the learning of no traditional content. Such an anti-intellectual stance is hardly what such originators of late twentieth-century paradigms as Michel Foucault, Mikhail Bakhtin, and Jacques Derrida had in mind. The most obviously anti-art, Jessie Helms-type rhetoric clearly postures for political gain. While posturing a contrasting concern for art, many self-styled practitioners of outlooks like deconstruction and post-structuralism are similarly anti-art and anti-intellectual. They often react with consternation and McCarthyism when presented with such points. Care for art is only pretense, masking crass political demands for power and visibility that are no less cynical in nature, and indeed actually less honest, than those of the disciples of Buchanan and Helms.

Beyond such artless and spiritually devolving discussions of the likes of Eakins, Melville and Ives onto the pedestrian facts of their race, ethnicity, and gender, other Americans continue, more fundamentally, to question their having any significance at all in American history beyond their own artistic circles. Some relativist and obscurantist discussions of many late twentieth-century academics lend legitimacy to such a perspective—that such a view has validity by simple virtue of its popularity. While there is always room merely to decry such views as anti-intellectual and indicative of a decay in American culture, the historical fact is that variations on such views have always been present in American history. American culture contains many elements which regularly contest the centrality of its own content. It has also had, in part as a convenient response to such troublesome contesting, a significant strain of thought which doubts, and at times rejects, the significance of the arts in the nation's life. While the European nations have had elite classes which have supported fine arts, the United States has had far less of this tradition, and the non-elites in America have often been ambivalent at best with respect to many of the arts. As a consequence of that ambivalence, the role of government in the arts in American has always been limited. Since 1964, with the National Endowments for the Arts and Humanities, the government has played some significant role. But even here the role has been minor compared with the norms of the major European nations. In 1988, for example, the then West German government spent four times the amount the U.S. government allotted for the arts, and in total, not merely per capita. Additionally, throughout the years of support, under the National Endowments as well as under earlier initiatives, Helms-like blasts of criticism have played significant roles in the political scene.

The question of public support for the arts has arisen repeatedly in American politics. Justifications have abounded, as have rationales for neglect, benign or otherwise. Judgments aside, the history of advocating or opposing systems of government support of the arts is an important component of American cultural history. In various forms the subject repeatedly arose in Congress. As it did changes occurred in the substantive focus of proposed legislation and in the content of the debates. The course of the changes reflects many key developments of American thought. The history of these efforts at establishing government arts programs constitutes a public history of Americans' thoughts on culture.

Virtually every Western nation has some sort of department or ministry of culture. For the sake of the state or religion, for ostentation, for the promotion of patriotism or creed, leaders have regarded the arts to be an important source of cultural reification to make abstract sensibilities more vibrant and concrete. Thus their promotion has had collective as well as individual value. Among major Western governments, the United States has shown the least interest in such an agency. In contrast to Europe, the United States has had no such traditional authorities as a national church, a monarchy, or nearly as entrenched or pervasive an aristocratic class, which have all been significant purveyors of culture. While such traditions were weaker in America, the issue of the arts in public policy has still had a persistent presence. Some efforts for government support of the arts have succeeded, most notably the Arts Projects of the New Deal's Works Progress Administration, and the current National Endowments. The minor successes and the many legislative failures in the history of this topic merit study along with the well-known successes. For the arguments surrounding these efforts reveal much about developing American attitudes toward the arts, toward the life of the mind, and toward America's cultural self-image.

To research the topic of debates over government and the arts, in addition to reading the myriad of published books, journal, periodical, and newspaper articles pertaining to all aspects of the subject, I examined the entire published Records and Indexes of the United States Congress and the accompanying Serial Sets, which catalogue all pertinent committee hearings and reports. In this endeavor, I am grateful to Mr. David Kepley and Mr. Robert Coren of the National Archives for their most helpful assistance. I am equally grateful to colleagues Paul Boyer of the University of Wisconsin and Richard von Mayrhauser of Slippery Rock University, who provided thoughtful insights and criticisms during phases of the preparation of this manuscript.

The Colonial and Early National Heritage

A lexis de Tocqueville once commented that the opinions of America's first fathers left very deep traces in the minds of their descendants. Several aspects of thought rooted in the Colonial period favored artistic and intellectual pursuits. Others tended to support neglect.

The heritage of Puritanism was a most important element in the American view of esthetics. Contrary to popular mythology, of course, the Puritans were intensely interested in esthetics and quite sensitive to beauty. Beauty and culture were no mere adornments to Puritan life, but they could not be pursued as ends in themselves. Truth could not be sought through beauty alone. Feeling and imagination could not fly freely. They had to operate within a theological framework, which required a trained intellect in order to fathom its meanings. That which lay beyond intellectually knowable theology was to be cleaved unto and loved. It was blasphemy to fancy that the cosmos could then be expressed through human sentiment or embodied through fancy. The opposite was open to contemporaneous artists under the aegis of the Catholic church and under that of less severe Protestant denominations. For the kind of artist who thrived in an environment which gave free reign to the expression of sensibilities, Puritanism thus appeared barren and cold. It was unacceptable to believe an artist could express a vision of reality that could resonate within all who witnessed it. The Puritans articulated the explicit unity of life's elements within a Divine order. No one of those elements, including, indeed especially an art, could transcend this. While their Catholic contemporaries enjoyed often exquisite liturgical music and visual representations of religious subjects on canvases, the Puritans expressly avoided such expression. In music, for example, the Puritans encouraged singing ("Make a joyful noise unto the Lord. Enter his gates singing with praise."). But they intentionally avoided the finely honed tunes they knew too well among their English rivals. "God's altar needs not our polishings," wrote Reverend Joseph Cotton, embodying the spirit of the Puritans avoidance not of esthetics but of esthetics divorced from a moral practice and stricture. Thus the Puritans often sang cacophonously, painted crudely (though not always), and opposed most excesses of ornamentation that potentially diverted the human soul from its only true attenuation.

While esthetics as an end in itself was blasphemy to any good Puritan, equally abhorrent was an anti-esthetic perspective. The former lost sight of the totality of the Kingdom of which esthetics were a part. The latter denied the existence of esthetics, thus attempting the impossible—the limiting of God's infinite wisdom. It was not that good Puritans chose to lead esthetically as well as ethically righteous lives, they simply could do no other. The Puritans thus had a fervent theological base for the recognition of the arts but only as a legitimate part of a complete moral life which sought to cleave unto all God's beauty. They adorned their lives of worship, within limits, and appreciated the beautiful achievements of others.

Long after Puritanism's decline arts and esthetics would be an integral element of the world view of such descendants as the Transcendentalists, who would celebrate much of what the Puritans worshiped. What lay within Puritanism which supported the glorification of man in art continued. The negative aspects of Puritanism which distrusted some forms of free expression in art had fallen away as the social and political strength of the religion faded before a more plural society and before liberal, democratic ideals. Puritan fervor remained a key component in the major transcendental movement of the early nineteenth century. While the Puritans worshiped God outside of Nature and saw Nature as a wilderness to be crafted by Man, the transcendentalists celebrated God in Nature and saw in the arts means of capturing this vision.[1] The arts provided a philosophical base for the lives of the famous Transcendentalist writers. Others of the time like Brook Farmer and critic John Sullivan Dwight sought to embody the same philosophical visions in musical analysis. In the same context, music later provided a broader philosophical end for the composer Charles Ives, who (though some question his claim) regarded himself a true esthetic descendent of Emerson and Thoreau. In a studied, retiring manner, the self-confessed "last Puritan" George Santayana found in esthetics a refuge upon which to build a moral system. His contemporary John Dewey considered esthetic questions to be an indispensable element in the panorama of issues which he sought to subject to systematic coherence. The line of American intellectual and cultural history which emanates out of Puritanism to the Great Awakening, to the Revolution, to Transcendentalism, to Pragmatism, and on into this century is shot through with issues of esthetics, but in a manner and tone which always sought a union of esthetics and ethics rather than entertaining the perceived suffusion of art for art's sake.

At the same time, outside of this New England-based tradition, a more utilitarian strain that originated in the seventeenth and eighteenth centuries held the arts and esthetics to be more diversionary in purpose. The arts were not neglected, but were regarded as adornments or escapes. Such prominent eighteenth-century Americans as Benjamin Franklin and Thomas Jefferson dabbled in the arts. As strong proponents of Enlightenment ideals, they linked the arts to a range of eclectic activities with which cultivated ladies and gentlemen should be acquainted. Their views on esthetics and the arts had no strong theological grounding. For Franklin they had little explicit linkage to his thought in other areas. Jefferson made more of an attempt to draw into a harmonious unit the many activities that caught his fancy, but it was often a highly personal and at times somewhat hazy vision. Beyond the tenuous cohesiveness of these non-New England esthetic traditions, the general diffusion and attenuation of different components of the life of the mind in eighteenth and early nineteenth-century America further disrupted their coherence. The social changes of the Revolution that culminated in Jacksonianism undermined old class characteristics of American culture and politics and replaced them with a loosely linked number of functional elites, no less elitist, but decidedly less artistic.[2]

The arts in early America generally had connections with life's tasks but were at best implicitly and not systematically linked to them. Utilitarianism predominated. Seventeenth and eighteenth-century governments, at the colonial or municipal level, did nothing for the arts. The arts were diversions, best left to to peoples' private lives. New York City was something of an exception. Its government, for example, supported the design and construction of several statues and monuments: a famous one was erected to George III to celebrate the 1766 repeal of the Stamp Act. During the Revolution it was melted down to make bullets.

The Revolution itself provided the one potential source of historical reference to American culture. But beyond the private and local domain, the early years of the Republic saw little art employing Revolutionary themes. The first monuments to George Washington were not erected until after the War of 1812. The only popular patriotic song of the late eighteenth, early nineteenth century was "Yankee Doodle," and it was written during the Revolution. "America the Beautiful," "America," and of course "The Star Spangled Banner" came during and after the War of 1812. The unison of national mourning upon the death of Washington in 1799 and the mass turnout for the funeral of Benjamin Franklin in 1790 (20,000, almost the entire population of Philadelphia) reveal cultural underpinnings to which a sensitive artist could give shape and meaning. Private artistic activity abounded in prints, ceramics, tapestries and songs. Yet no artist seemed willing or able to grasp this and give reification in any grand form. Any "genius" theory of art history would simply have it that no one of requisite capability and inspiration happened to come along at that moment. Seeing the arts in a social context and not in a vacuum, however, reveals the effects of key political dynamics.

The issue of government support of the arts could have arisen during the drafting and ratification of the Constitution. As educated men of the eighteenth-century Enlightenment, the Founding Fathers knew that European governments had supported science and the arts, and their sensibilities held all areas of learning in high esteem. At the Constitutional Convention James Madison mentioned the possibility of creating a National University. Charles Coatesworth Pinckney wanted to "establish seminaries for the promotion of literature and the arts and sciences." But the proposals failed. John Adams' dictum, "I study war so my children can study politics, so their children can study art," bespoke a sense of the integration of esthetics, morality and life, but set some clear priorities as well. The Federalists wanted stronger central government than did their opponents, but they still feared the growth of National power. And as they worked for the ratification of the Constitution, they did not want any nonessential component of their document to serve as a point around which criticism of National power could cohere.[3]

Aside from the construction of some statues and other adornments for buildings in Washington, largely under Jefferson, no official measures regarding the arts were taken during the early years of the Republic. The Constitution allows the promotion of "the Progress of Science and useful Arts." But endeavors along these lines, conceived then largely via favorable copyright and patent laws, fell victim to the jealousies between the states and their representatives which raged over such key issues as tariffs, the National Bank, and the construction of roads and canals. In 1790 representatives could not be cajoled into voting funds for scientific studies of the yellow fever plaguing the capital of Philadelphia that year. The famous British chemist Joseph Priestley had expressed confidence that the spirit of the Republic would remove obstructions from the exertion of all kinds of talent and prove "far more favorable to science and to the arts than any mechanical government had ever been."[4] At the very least, his optimism was premature. Only a few efforts took place at the state level to support education and for the creation of museums and learned institutions.

At the Federal level, the promotion of learned societies, such as Philadelphia's American Philosophical Society, fell under the rubric of "internal improvements." Debates over this subject provide a window onto the early leaders' views on the question of government responsibility and suitability for involvement in the promotion of intellect and more generally in regard to the creative process and the life of the mind. Further, the issue touched on the question of the negative image of Europe in many Americans' minds who have in turn opposed many forms of government activity in the arts. In 1790, Rep. Roger Sherman of Connecticut successfully argued that since the idea of a National University had been rejected, Congress could not legitimately create any other such scientific or general institution of learning. The early Presidents all had ideas about national efforts for culture and learning however. From Washington to John Quincy Adams, each President continued to toy with the idea of a university in the nation's capital. Justifications focused on the desirability of drawing talent together for the national good, lest New England's bright young men remain at Harvard and Yale and budding Jeffersons stay in the South. Localism won out in each debate.

During the second Washington administration came several opportunities to pursue the establishment of a National university. Washington favored the creation of a national center of learning, fearing the "dissipation and extravagance" that could come from European education and wishing to counter any excesses of localism and regional jealousies. Washington promised to fund a National University by donating all his shares in the Potomac Canal Company and in the James River Canal Company. This was laid before the Congress. A somewhat contrasting possibility emerged in 1795 when a group of university professors from Geneva suddenly found themselves in limbo, as political revolution had removed their government, hence their financial support. Vice President

John Adams and, even more, Thomas Jefferson were intrigued with the idea. Jefferson tried unsuccessfully to interest the Virginia legislature in such an intellectual importation. An exchange of letters between the estranged Washington and Jefferson reflected their contrasting visions regarding how and to what end a national university could be established. Jefferson envisioned the Genevans and others situated in Virginia, just outside the future District of Columbia. Washington feared potential aristocratic tendencies from a European faculty and preferred an American institution in the Federal city. The Geneva idea went nowhere. In 1796 Congress did entertain the possibility of creating a National University from the nation's own resources. That too failed. In December, 1796 a vote to postpone all debate passed by but thirty-seven to thirty-six. Jefferson certainly remained interested in the promotion of learning. Beyond the obvious fact of his founding of the the University of Virginia, his interest in "high" culture certainly revealed itself during his Presidency. The adornments with which he graced the new Presidential residence were the finest he could procure. He hired Italian sculptors to provide many works for the White House. In 1807 Jefferson considered advocating a national philosophical society. The strength of his political base had eroded during his second term, however, and tensions over relations with Britain and France and the Chesapeake affair shortly ensued. The idea then had to be shelved.[5]

Of the early Presidents John Quincy Adams was the strongest proponent of a national university. Indeed his Presidency marked the peak of an eighteenth-century sensibility which wanted Washington D.C. to become another Paris and America to follow European models with regard to government and culture. Adams' would be a lonely voice.[6]

The Republic had begun with a rejection of the Articles of Confederation and the passage of the Constitution. The question of the degree of central authority in a Republic went to the heart of the debate over the acceptability of the new government. Once begun, the Constitutional government's leaders were wary of fulfilling the fears of anti-Federalist critics and were thus reluctant to engage in any excesses of centralization, particularly if any such efforts appeared to embrace European ways. National academies, universities, and learned and artistic societies all presented such specters of decadence, effeteness and corruption. Regional suspicions from within the government greatly added to the patterns of reluctance and opposition.

Notes

1. see Perry Miller, *"From Edwards to Emerson," Errand in the Wilderness* (Harvard University Press, 1956, and Paul Conkin, *Puritans and Pragmatists* (Indiana University Press, 1968).

2. see, for example, John Bach McMaster, *Benjamin Franklin as a Man of Letters,* New York: Arno Press, 1970; *Jefferson and the Arts,* Washington: National Gallery of Art, 1976; Helen Cripe, *Thomas Jefferson and Music,* Charlottesville: University Press of Virginia, 1974, and Stow Persons, *The Decline of American Civility.*

3. Max Farrand, *The Records of the Federal Convention of 1787* (New Haven: Yale University Press, 1911-1937), II, p. 325.

4. E.F. Smith, *Priestley in America, 1794-1804* (Philadelphia, 1920), p. 50.

5. *The Debates and Proceedings of the Congress of the United States, Washington:* Gales and Seaton, 1834 and 1852: 1st Congress, 2d Session, 1790, p. 1551; 2d Congress, 1792, p. viii; 4th Congress, 2d Session, 1796, pp. 1600-01, 1672, 1694, 1697, 1704, 1708, and 1711; 7th Congress, 2d Session, 1802, pp. 345-46; 9th Congress, 1st Session, 1805, p. 301; 2d Session, 1806, p. 426; see also, James Thomas Flexner, *George Washington: Anguish and Farewell, 1793-1799.* (Boston: Little Brown and Co., 1972), pp. 199-202; Niel Harris, *The Artist in America* (New York: G.Braziller, 1966), passim.; Irving Bryant, *James Madison* (Indianapolis: Indiana University Press, 1941-50), III, pp. 447-48; and Hunter DuPree, *Science in the Federal Government, A History of Policies and Activities to 1940* (Harvard, 1957), chapters 1 and 2.

6. see J. Sterling Young, *The Washington Community, 1800-1828* (New York, 1966) and David Schuyler, *The New Urban Landscape: The Redefinition of the City Form in Nineteenth-Century America* (Baltimore: Johns Hopkins University Press, 1986).

Public Policy and the Arts in the Jacksonian Era

While early Presidents and other leaders hotly debated the proper limits of Federal authority, none from Washington to John Quincy Adams disagreed with the concept of pooling intellectual talent for the national good. For a time after 1815, as antagonisms decreased between Republicans and what remained of the Federalists, it briefly seemed that a unified political/cultural state could emerge that would not unduly damage the interests and sensibilities of any particular region. John C. Calhoun's support of tariffs and of the rechartering of the National Bank are commonly cited examples of the degree to which nationalism for a time eclipsed sectional concerns. In the context of intellectual activities, Calhoun's work as head of the War Department in the Monroe Administration illustrates this further. For it was none less than Calhoun who was instrumental in transforming West Point from a desultory technical school into an intellectually formidable college à la Paris' Ecole Polytechnique, to that end appointing Sylvanus Thayer to be Commandant. At the private level there emerged national songs, monuments to Washington, and painting which sought to extol the beauty of American scenery.

But as visions of national unity swelled, so, too, did more particularistic views. Sectional antagonisms over the War of 1812, over banking, internal improvements, tariffs, and most of all slavery sowed seeds of discontent with regard to Federal authority. More generally, sentiments loosely labeled democratic, egalitarian and Jacksonian in the rising cities and in the West blared over the more carefully orchestrated tones of John Quincy Adams and his predecessors.

Amidst this rising new political style, older sensibilities faded. Of the intellectual vestiges of the Colonial heritage, those of Puritanism—Congregationalism and Unitarianism—faded somewhat in their social significance in the years immediately after the War of 1812. Until the rise of abolitionism and other reforms, more utilitarian strains of American traditions dominated politics. Distrust of national power, while always present, grew less discriminatory in character. Formally trained intellect fell from its exalted position among the virtues of leadership. At worst it became a liability, as a new anti-elitism swept older mores from political culture.

Many factors explain this transformation. With the democratization of the voting booth to include most free white Northern males by 1830, American politics changed. Voters remained deferential, but they deferred to new leaders. Tocqueville himself described this process as one in which society grew "more democratic, less brilliant."[1] Rather than shaping political sensibilities, politics more readily fell to their lowest common denominator. The appearance of learning ceased to be an asset for men running for public office. As Jackson said of one fired government worker: "he's fit to write a book and scarcely that." New leadership spoke out vigorously against established elites, and against the culture and regions to which those elites were linked. Intellectualism associated with that older leadership suffered. Sympathy for the life of the mind and for the philosopher as statesman fell away with the new wave of democracy in the 1820s and 1830s. Within fifteen years Congressmen switched concerns, literally and metaphorically, from the continued wearing of wigs to the carrying of knives.

As a loosely bound set of functionaries displaced a more unified set of leadership sensibilities a discernible ambivalence emerged in regard to certain issues, previously considered of great importance, that demanded a carefully honed, singular sense of purpose. In this vein, for example, the fate of urban planning in the nation's capital suffered measurably. Unplanned growth and privatization found easy rationalization. Washington, D.C., as Henry Adams noted, "developed into a mean, slatternly place virtually no one found attractive." Charles Dickens saw "spacious avenues that begin in nothing and lead nowhere ... public buildings that need but a public to be complete and ornaments of great thoroughfares which lack only great thoroughfares to ornament."[2] Washington, D.C. could thus neither become a center of national culture nor subsequently provide a basis for any national activism in the genres of culture. The effects of this rapid transformation of leadership sensibilities revealed themselves most dramatically in John Quincy Adams' term as President. Much that he proposed was rejected, although virtually all of it would later come to fruition: a Department of the Interior, a Naval Academy, a National Astronomical Laboratory, a system of weights and measures, government aid to various intellectual and artistic endeavors. Staunch supporters like William Wirt felt Adams' proposals somewhat bold. Friend Henry Clay believed the dream of a National University "entirely hopeless" and conceded "there was something in the Constitutional objection to it."[3] Aware of potential resistance from the new espousers of fashionable democratic rhetoric,

Adams implored Congressmen not to be "palsied by the wills of ... constituents."[4] The notion that the common people lacked any sort of will was abhorrent to rising democratic sensibilities. With such rhetoric, Adams's opponents could not have been given a greater gift, and they defeated virtually everything he proposed. The President's tonality accentuated his opponents' vehemence. Some Congressmen proposed a Constitutional amendment "to place beyond the power of Congress to make surveys, construct roads, establish a National University, and to offer and distribute prizes for promoting agriculture, education, science, and the liberal and useful arts."[5] Notions of the primacy of intellect and the legitimacy of its support by government stood against the onrush of anti-elitism, states' rights and regionalism. Adams' proposals for support of scientific and artistic learning were abandoned with little remorse and more than a little glee.

In the midst of this political shift away from potential sympathy for the arts, American arts themselves were undergoing an efflorescence which had a certain affinity to the popular predelictions against government support. The Transcendentalist movement in literature and philosophy and the Hudson River School of painting were the most famous points of American cultural growth in the early and mid-nineteenth century. Both sought to become something more that an offshoot of European culture. Like the new political leaders, such artists and writers as Thomas Cole and Ralph Waldo Emerson each believed that Americans needed to be conscious of their personal and collective roots to achieve greatness and were better off forsaking European finery.

Ironically, this artistic quest for a national inner spirit independent of Europe paralleled aspects of the Romantic movement in Europe. Immanuel Kant's "categorical imperative," via the poetry of William Wordsworth and Samuel Taylor Coleridge, had an underlying kinship with Emerson's "oversoul." The American turn to native themes and genres had its counterpart in the German discovery of the Volk. Irony aside, like the Romantics across the Atlantic, the American Transcendentalists believed any imposed structure restricted the well-springs of creativity which, as Emerson reflected, were best developed through self reliance. To the extent that they then formulated a political ideology, Transcendentalists were radically Jeffersonian, strongly holding to the ideals of minimal government and individuality.

Some artists did not object to the notion of government support, however limited that support might be. Government commissions, largely those to decorate various parts of the Capitol Building, provided a spiritually and intellectually uplifting alternative to the boring private market of portraiture that had been the artists' mainstay. The government support could prompt works to regenerate patriotic spirits; Washington could be filled with reminders in paint and stone of the sacrifices and glories of the past. Political leaders could begrudgingly accept this general concept. The particular subjects to be employed in such art prompted acrimonious debates, however. With regional jealousies a generalized patriotism seemed the only safe topic. In 1817 when Congress appropriated funds to employ artists to create the works for the Rotunda and other spots of the Capitol the vote was 114 to 50. The opposition voiced the principle of no government involvement. Others said no such spending should occur until the war debt is paid. Some wanted to see the paintings first. The Vicar of Wakefield, it was noted, once commissioned a portrait which turned out so large it could not fit into his home. Others simply rejected the argument that patriotism could be enhanced and held that paintings could have no inspirational value to the spirit of defending freedom. "Rights and liberties," asserted one Congressmen, "depend on no such paltry considerations as those of a mere painting."[6]

Political jealousies ran through the debates over the paintings in the 1820s. The cliques linked to the old Federalists and future Whigs largely favored the work. Proto-Jacksonians generally opposed it, though, for example, the generally Jacksonian Rep. James Hamilton supported the venture in hopes of securing favorable employment for his fellow South Carolinian Washington Allston. The issue of appropriate subjects for the paintings prompted much conflict. Some Jacksonians naturally wanted the Battle of New Orleans, for example. Northern anti-Jacksonians preferred some of the naval battles on Lake Erie. Jacksonian Congressmen George Kremmer then suggested sardonically that one of the paintings ought to portray the Hartford Convention. As the topics of paintings were engulfed in political rivalries, painters found themselves in some nasty crossfires over which they had no power, very much like the artists pilloried by the political right wing of the late twentieth century.[7]

In regard to the question of suitability, the Revolution seemed the only subject upon which most Congressmen could agree. Representative Henry Wise of Virginia, upset with the pettiness involved in the arguments over subjects for paintings, threw up his hands and asserted that a focus purely on pre-1789 subjects was the only means to avoid bickering.[8] Government officials to whom artists appealed for commissions developed narrow views as to what history was appropriate. Colonial themes such as Bacon's Rebellion, the Glorious Revolution against Gov. Andros, and the founding of the House of Burgesses exemplified the heritages of resistance to injustice and of representative government. Each could have merited artistic treatment, and a depiction of the Glorious Revolution does hang in the Massachusetts House of Representatives. But in the early and mid nineteenth century such topics generated sectional and religious controversies. John Chapman's Capitol painting The Baptism of Pocohontas prompted one comment in 1855: "it is unworthy of the artist, of the position it occupies, and the Government to which it belongs."[9] In 1823 Congress balked at painter Julia Planton's request for remuneration for her portrait of the negotiators of the Treaty of Ghent that ended the War of 1812. The Committee on Public Buildings contended Constitutional grounds were lacking.[10]

The Capitol paintings receiving the most attention were those of John Trumbull on the surrenders of Burgoyne and Cornwallis, on *The Resignation of General Washington*, and, most strongly, *The Declaration of Independence*. Even though the topics were politically safe, they were the first paintings commissioned, so no opponent had yet grown weary of voicing opposition. Additionally the paintings' premiers occurred in the late 1820s, at the adolescent height of the proto-Whig/ Jacksonian rivalry. The result was resentful sniping from many opposed to any government spending along such lines as the arts. Trumbull received $32,000 for his four paintings. To this Senator John Holmes of Maine, to whom Thomas Jefferson had earlier written his "Fire Bell in the Night" letter, scoffed that the four paintings were not worth thirty-two cents. Representative William McCoy's response to them was yet more blunt: viewing the results of Trumbull's publicly sponsored labors, he mused, "if the Fine Arts cannot thrive in this country without government jobs ... let them fail." Most famously, John

Randolph of Virginia reportedly doubled over in laughter at *The Declaration of Independence*. In its original form, the painting presented the rows of Continental Congressmen all in knee breeches with almost militarily aligned crossed legs. Randolph thus mocked it "a shin piece; ... never before was such a collection of legs submitted to the eyes of man."[11] Randolph's comment was typical of his clever, though often vacuous, panache. His response did cause Trumbull ultimately to cover the various shins by painting clothed tables in front of several Congressmen, as the work (and the back of a two dollar bill) now displays.

Randolph's caustic remarks also prompted Trumbull to engage in a fantasy correspondence with the caustic Virginian. He intended to publish a note to Randolph, referring to him as one "so very like a yellow pippin shrivelled with a winter's keeping," lamenting that Randolph's "elegant education and ample fortune might have rendered him an eminent patron and protector of the fine arts." Fantasizing a subsequent challenge to a duel, Trumbull prepared an answer:

> I have done with fighting ... the day after the Siege of New Port was raised [1778] ... it would be a very silly thing for an Old Man of seventy-two—somewhat portly ... to expose himself in single combat with a young gentleman whose elegant slender figure affords no better mark for a pistol ball than a stripped cornstalk. There would be no reciprocity in such a Contest.

As Trumbull's biographer noted: "The 'logomachy' to which Trumbull proceeded to challenge Randolph as an alternative to the 'duel' ... would certainly have been well matched: had it taken place American letters would have enriched by a fine chapter in epistolary warfare."[12]

Given the visibility of such public supported artistic activity as painting for the Capitol, and with the barbs that often resulted, artists of the era often shied from the controversial. While the political battles of the day forced artists' historical consciousness onto a precious tutelage to the Revolution, many felt it wise to ignore history altogether. Americans' sense of history was generally limited, some philosophers like Emerson implied it a point of superiority not to be mired in the past. Americans' experiences could not be considered with anyone else's.

Aware of the political minefield around them, some artists contended, or rationalized, that the sources of Americans' creative processes to be unlike those of European artists. They believed America to be an egalitarian society which had transcended decadent Europe. Emerson,

Hawthorne and other writers indeed felt Europe offered them few inspirations. Painters like Washington Allston and Thomas Cole claimed to have garnered technique there but little else. While in Europe tensions between nations, classes, religions and other contending forces inspired many creative activities, America allegedly had none of this. Such American painters as Allston and Rembrandt Peale never employed American historical subjects in their works. American artists generally drew upon more serene, purportedly higher spiritual sources. When they gave testimony to this view they curried political favor. Charles Sumner, for example, praised Washington Allston's sense that no military battle or, more generally, "no scene of human strife can find a place in the highest art."[13]

On the other hand, when Trumbull's *Declaration of Independence* was unveiled at the Capitol in 1825, John Quincy Adams found the work troubling because it appeared to him utterly devoid of strife and tension. One need but glance at the rather blank expressions in the eyes of Jefferson, Adams, Franklin, Hancock (perhaps appropriate in his case), and the other delegates to grasp John Quincy Adams' reservations. President Adams was revealing his usual sensibilities, attuned more to pure intellect than to political realities, a proclivity which often placed him out of step with many of his day. Given the momentous nature of the event that Adams was viewing on Trumbull's canvas, "tension" was to him a most salient emotional feature. Generally Trumbull's canvasses do evince a rather flattened character. Adams indeed grasped what would become the professional critical community's general view of Trumbull. Due to a fall at age five, Trumbull was sightless in his left eye and thus could not see or impart that depth which Adams felt necessary to the scene of 1776. Utterly concerned with the intellectually verifiable truth of the matter at hand, Adams was academically right. But he was politically out of touch. A flattened facsimile on the subject of the Revolution was the politically safe path of the day. Trumbull's proclivities fit well, and he achieved success. Deploring the critics, particularly Randolph's "unscrupulous sarcasm," Horatio Greenough encapsulated the generally favorable reaction to Trumbull as he intoned: "I believe I shall be speaking the sense of the artistical body, and of the cognoscenti in the United States, when I say that *The Declaration of Independence* has earned the respect of all."[14]

Trumbull's depthless views of history and Washington Allston's dictum that combat had no place in high art conveniently fit the political climate of an era into which John Quincy Adams' temperament could not.

Any resulting spiritual torpor in art was a potentiality easily mortgaged. Surrounded by political crossfires, the artistic community appeared to seek serenity. This sentiment combined with regional jealousies that left few "safe" topics of history, with the broader anti-institutional perspective inherent in transcendentalism, and with the utilitarian views of public officials, to constrict severely the prospects for public support of the arts as well as the degree to which many artists and politicians would seek it.

The belief in artistic inspiration, devoid of tension and reflective of serenity, illustrated an optimism in an Emerson or a Cole. Both held the United States to be a new, pure nation that could accept history as a given and not feel compelled to grapple with it. This would not easily resonate within an individual capable of doubt, i.e., with a sense of history. That sense tends to come in cultures which have been chastened by tragedy. For early nineteenth-century Americans the only perceived suffering seemed to lie beyond their shores (since few yet cared about slaves or Indians). Free of such baggage, life involved steady progress and outward spiritual serenity.

Nathaniel Hawthorne and Herman Melville were the major exceptions to this optimistic stance among the American writers led by Emerson and Thoreau. Representing the darker side of transcendentalism, Hawthorne and Melville accepted Emerson's view of the alienation that nineteenth-century urbanization and industrialization brought to the soul, but did not share Emerson's positive sense that solutions were readily available. Americans seemed to prefer the optimistic view. In his lifetime Melville thus generally enjoyed more popularity in Europe than in the United States (as did the native and historically oriented novels of James Fenimore Cooper). Right or wrong, the general tone of American artists before the Civil War involved unqualified optimism, with a minimal belief in society's need for historical grounding. The use of the arts by government to enhance historical depth and sensitivity was thus limited. And the philosophical underpinning of the American artistic and literary worlds held the best government to be minimal.

A broader problem with which artists had to contend involved what it meant to be an American. Compared to their European counterparts, their social functions as artists were unclear. Artists were then diverted by questions of personal and professional definition. An art-for-art's-sake attitude was one resolution. But this did not mesh with the self-consciously nationalistic and democratic culture of nineteenth-century America. A society in which artists worried only about art and left political and social questions to politicians and journalists seemed more European in character, though certainly not the only artistic tradition of Europe. It allowed a certain elite to grapple with key political issues. This flew in the face of various American traditions. The Puritans were uncomfortable with such earthly hierarchies, though they certainly employed them. At their best they struggled incessantly against any such earthly hierarchy growing *sui generis*. The Jeffersonian ideal called upon all citizens to be politically active and vigilant against elite encroachments upon liberty. The contemporary transcendentalist self-reliant vision saw every man as his own philosopher. Any mechanistic division of the appropriate functions of citizens was thus unacceptable. Devoid of any European class system which, at its best, gave protection to the pure artist, American democracy placed the socially responsible artist in a new position for which no resolution had been forged. American artists were then compelled to think about their work and its function rather than just create it. Such diversions can prove debilitating.

Only later, with the rise of the anti-slavery movement, did Transcendentalism imply an esthetic which could be conjoined to a political vision to help advocate a better society. Transcendentalists came to see that moral judgments could be bases for political action and that esthetic visions could similarly constitute not mere standards by which to judge society's health but blueprints to enhance it. But because of the priority of political and social reform, this new esthetic view paradoxically remained dormant until after the Civil War.[15]

Throughout the years from the end of the War of 1812 to the Civil War, the views of artists on their proper role in national affairs and on the issue of official support of their work rattled amidst the din of national politics. Ambivalence predominated, and many politicians were hostile to the arts in general and detested expenditures on murals and other works for the Capitol. Culture and the arts assumed a place not unlike that of Indians—noble, disposable, best left to state, local and private authority.

Rarely in the nineteenth century did any substantive initiatives for the arts pass in Congress. Americans, as Charles Dickens said, were busy. On the surface this description is both trite and stupefying. Yet so many notable foreign travellers who wrote about America in this era, from Dickens, to Tocqueville, to Frances Trolloppe, made such observations. Preoccupied with "everyday" concerns, American politicians put the arts on a back burner. Sentiment against officialdom, in any form, directing and shaping American life heightened opposition to the view that Federally sponsored arts could raise the public spirit and deepen patriotism. The creative arts were fine, but they belonged in private hands with the government doing nothing. In 1839, for example, sculptor Hiram Powers returned from a stay in Italy. He had to pay $600 in duties for a marble statue on which he had been working. In the context of tariffs, the government made no distinction between art and slabs of stone, and Powers's petition for an exception to be made on the basis of such a distinction was rejected.[16]

As a consequence of the "private" ideal, the arts in mid nineteenth-century America reflected growing geographical and class divisions in the society. The urban upper class dominated the world of the fine or cultivated arts. But many popular vernacular traditions grew as well, distinct from and at times in conscious opposition to cultivated traditions. Antagonism between the cultivated and vernacular elite/non-elite spheres, often as much rhetorical as real, created a climate in which the idea of any sort of public support of arts aroused suspicions and jealousies. The visibility of the cultivated urban upper class art world made it the most likely beneficiary of any such program. This would play into the hands of any skilled politician whose support lay with the vernacular. With the anti-elitist rhetorical success of the Jacksonians against Adams and the co-option of their posture by the Whigs, the cultivated arts of American life stood well on the periphery. The division between the cultivated and vernacular genres of the arts grew in virtually all fields. Little commerce took place between them, owing in part to the government's absence, which left nineteenth-century American culture less anchored.

The lack of a singular and unifying national culture was not necessarily evil. Indeed the argument of some of the founding fathers (in the tenth Federalist paper, for example), held that cultures, revealed by political parties, would not emerge on a national level. While no such unifying culture was emerging, the principal political climate taking hold with Jackson and the co-opting Whigs had pronounced strain of anti-intellectualism. In such an atmosphere government efforts were minimal and usually but vaguely related to the arts. More paintings and statues were purchased for the Capitol. The legitimacy of tariffs on foreign art and on musical instruments received some discussion, but generally the duties rose steadily. In 1836 Congress provided funds for American participation in three conventions in Brussels, Bern, and Rome which focused on the development of international copyright laws in literature and art. The funding was minimal, and the focus was more legal than artistic. (The failure to reach any international accord here and elsewhere, incidentally, was a chief motive for Charles Dickens's subsequent tour of the United States during which he sought, with little success, to untangle various copyright matters with American publishers.)[17]

A significant Congressional expenditure of $20,000 for statuary during the Jacksonian era was allocated for Horatio Greenough's *George Washington,* a work intended as the centerpiece of the Capitol Rotunda. As with the paintings for the Capitol Building and with the debates over the idea of a National University, cosmopolitan, European-oriented sensibilities clashed with the rough-hewn anti-elitism which had catapulted Jackson to power. Greenough's statue, which he created in Europe, cast Washington in toga-like minimal cloth garb, virtually bare-chested. A few praised it—"Sublime!" extolled Samuel F.B. Morse, for example. But many viewers were shocked. The pertinence of Classical casting was (and remains ever more) lost on most who wanted to see in George Washington their George Washington. For most this could not be a Periclean figure but a man of the people. Americans with ties to European high-culture were an ever diminishing political voice. Outrage grew. Defenses of the work could only intensify the anger. Rumors flew that the huge fifteen-foot statue threatened to sink the ship which transported it back from Italy and would do similar damage to the Capitol Building. Ultimately, Congress abandoned the plan to place George Washington in the Rotunda. The statue was consigned to the Smithsonian, here very much earning its epithet, "the nation's attic."[18]

The establishment of the Smithsonian Institution constituted one significant government initiative in regard to the arts in the nineteenth century. While significant in its many specific endeavors to the present day, the nature of the Institute's founding itself illustrates the ambivalence with which the government felt about the arts.

James Smithson died with but one heir—a nephew who himself passed away in 1835 leaving no heirs. Smithson's will left his estate, valued at just over a half million dollars ($508,318.46) to the United States "to found at Washington . . . an establishment for the increase and diffusion of knowledge among men." After some legal jousts in England where the nephew lived, yielding his mother a lifetime yearly stipend of £150, the United States government then considered how to dispose of the legacy. John C. Calhoun led a small group of Senators opposing the acceptance of the gift at all. "Acting under this legacy," he asserted "would be as much the establishment of a national university as if they appropriated money for the purpose. . . . It is beneath the dignity of the

United States to receive presents of this kind from anyone." Equating a National University with the hated National Bank, Thomas Hart Benton of Missouri joined Calhoun here. But the move for an outright decline of the gift failed by a vote of thirty-one to seven.[19] The government then spent eleven years debating what to do with the gift. The structure of the government left no clear means by which the gift could be spent. Senator Asher Robbins of Rhode Island introduced resolutions for the establishment to be a scientific and literary institution. Calhoun and Benton rose again and secured defeat of the proposal twenty to fifteen.[20] A Congressional committee led by John Quincy Adams, then a Representative from Massachusetts, gained charge of the matter. They debated among themselves and suffered hoards of what Adams dubbed "hungry and worthless political jackals." They entertained serious ideas including Adams's old dream of a National University, but in 1846 the committee settled on the idea of a multi-faceted gallery. In August, 1846 the Senate passed the enabling legislation twenty-six to thirteen; the House by but eighty-five to seventy-six. Were it not for the pressing concerns over the impending war with Mexico, the measure may have failed. In addition to the formidability of the opposition that considered such activities beyond the legitimate scope of the Federal Government, the omnibus nature of the Smithsonian's operation, which continues to the present day, with an overseeing board comprised of the Vice President, the Chief Justice, and Congressionally appointed citizens, illustrates how the structure of the national government could not smoothly accommodate the genres of learning and of the arts and sciences. Like the architecture of its main "castle" building, the Smithsonian was an oddity in 19th-century Washington, as Mark Twain dubbed it, "a poor, useless, innocent, mildewed old fossil, . . . collecting seeds and uncommon yams and extraordinary cabbages and peculiar bullfrogs."[21] The Smithsonian would actually be more than "America's attic," funding as it did some useful scientific research in the nineteenth century. Twain's jocularity did, however, very much encapsulate the general sentiment around him about this "fossil."

Significant action occurred in the 1840s when Congress approved an exchange of books, artifacts, and artistic and scientific materials with France. In the late eighteenth, early nineteenth century, Charles Wilson Peale had attempted exchanges between his Philadelphia Museum and European institutions and individuals, though the government was not involved. The official exchange of the 1840's was initiated and organized by a curious and rather charismatic Frenchman named Alexandre

Vattemare. Vattemare had had a most varied and colorful life up to this point—training in theology and surgery, and a successful performing career throughout Europe as a seance medium, ventriloquist, actor, mime, comedian and impersonator. The notables before whom he performed included Tsar Nicholas I of Russia, Prince Metternich of Austria, Sir Walter Scott and Goethe. Wherever he travelled in Europe, Vattemare visited museums and libraries and noted the waste of duplication. The Munich Library, he noted, held 200,000 duplicates, St. Petersburg's had 54,000, Vienna 30,000.[22] From those experiences he developed the idea that nations ought exchange their duplicates and enhance the collections of all interested parties. Vattemare successfully established such an exchange between Lisbon and St. Petersburg and expanded an existing one between Paris and London. In 1835 Vattemare proposed a general European exchange plan. In practical terms, he and his government were concerned about patent rights, scientific exchanges, international laws against scientific and commercial fraud, and the implantation of a metric system of weights and measures. Vattemare hoped for the establishment of a permanent international agency in Paris to oversee such commerce—with himself as director, of course.[23]

Vattemare was interested in drawing the United States and Canada into his system. James Smithson's gift to the United States inspired him.[24] Encouraged by the Marquis de Lafayette, Vattemare travelled in America from 1839 to 1841 and from 1847 to 1850, winning support for his program in Congress and in many state governments. In June, 1840 Congress' Joint Committee on the Library authorized the Librarian of Congress to exchange duplicates and see to it additional copies of documents were printed, all to be turned over to Vattemare.[25] Thirteen states set aside $100 to $400 to Vattemare for his work. Maine appropriated $1000. In 1840 and 1841 Louisiana allocated $6000. The cities of Montreal and Quebec each appropriated £5000. Vattemare also contacted officials in Mexico and Havana. The United States and the individual states sent to Vattemare nearly 2000 volumes, maps, coins and engravings and objects of art, science and natural history.[26] The American displays at the London Crystal Palace Exhibition of 1851 are commonly regarded as the point at which European leaders first took keen notice of American culture, yet, thanks to Vattemare, the French received similar material two years earlier.

Vattemare sent to the United States materials which covered a variety of fields in the arts and sciences. Three hundred thousand volumes crossed the ocean, and materials were received in every state east of the Mississippi and Missouri. French writers gave Vattemare volumes of their novels to try to stimulate interest in their work. (In order not to imperil his work among what he perceived to be rather prudish American sensibilities, Vattemare refused to accept any works from George Sand or Victor Hugo.) Vattemare gained significant support for his work. In addition to the subsidies he received from many states, railroads gave him free passage, and the federal government permitted all his materials from France to pass duty free.

That the government would support such a wide ranging program is curious in view of the anti-intellectualism of the era. But when the enabling proposals came before the Joint Congressional Committee on the Library of Congress in 1847, many legislators including Thomas Hart Benton, John Quincy Adams, Henry Clay and Daniel Webster wrote glowing letters of support. John Quincy Adams extolled Vattemare rhetorically:

> Go on with your great work. By it you are advancing the cause of civilization and improvement. ... people will not only exchange specimens of arts, literature and science, but they will intermit thoughts, ideas and sentiments.

Henry Clay declared:

> The plan of interchange proposed by Mr. Vattemare cannot fail to augment the knowledge, while it will cement the amicable relations of the nations adopting it. He is entitled to great praise for the arduous and disinterested exertions which he has made ... .

In his typically overblown rhetoric, Thomas Hart Benton wrote:

> I cannot limit myself to the expression of my great approbation of Mr. Vattemare's plan, and my sincere desire to see it accomplished. ...I feel it one of the felicities of my life to have had an opportunity of making the personal acquaintance of a gentleman who is the author and inventor of a scheme so enlarged and liberal, and so conducive to the good understanding of nations.

More floridly, Daniel Webster commented:

> Mr. Vattermare's conception is original, philanthropic and practical. It is worthy of the age and of the approbation of all enlightened men—the cry of the civilized world is that of Ajax:

> "(In Classical Greek) "Grant that my own eyes may behold."[27]

Support for the program stemmed, in part, from the fact that all sections of the nation took part, thus minimizing potential regional jealousies for which anti-intellectualism was often a mask. The Congressional Joint Committee on the Library indeed commented on the "great simplicity of the plan . . . and its utter separation from everything of a political and party character."[28] Such prominent private citizens as Washington Irving and Samuel F.B. Morse also lent support to Vattemare's efforts. The State of Pennsylvania declared "what LaFayette did for political liberty Vattemare does for intellectual pleasure and spiritual peace."[29]

The program's coordination by a Frenchman seemed to have preempted potential regional antagonisms. Had a Harvard-educated Bostonian attempted such an undertaking, resentment would have abounded. Vattemare rested beyond this. He was among the several Frenchmen who travelled in and wrote favorably of America.[30] He presaged Americans who benefitted in early twentieth-century Paris from the fascination of Frenchmen who were enchanted with American culture, while regarding their own provincials as boors. Perhaps a foreigner could be more esthetically objective and free of real as well as perceived sectional biases. Additionally, pedigree and personality likely outstripped any objective esthetic or scholarly sense with Vattemare.

The Vattemare experience demonstrates that at some level Americans fundamentally respected culture and intellect. Vattemare's efforts, wrote the *Southern Literary Messenger*, "set some in doubt of the old maxim, 'nothing liberal can be got from the rabble.'"[31] The anti-intellectual rhetoric to the contrary had real impact, however, and the resulting denial of esthetic and intellectual pleasure paradoxically served to heighten the urgency for cultural fulfillment. Careful, flattering approaches from unthreatening French sources could then have significant impact.

Vattemare's official reporting showed skill and political sensitivity along these lines. In his original report to the Joint Congressional Committee on the Library of Congress he appealed to the ego of American leaders, emphasizing how "eminent men everywhere greet with hope and enthusiasm an establishment which springs out of . . . your new soul-searching intellectual and political empire, calculated to concentrate the lustre of your intellectual sovereignty . . . to other nations of the world." Having long resented sneers from elite Easterners, Americans from "the heartland" enjoyed praise from a representative of an undisputed center of Western culture. The phrase "soul-searching intellectual empire" struck well at those distrustful of intellectualism as an end in itself, regardless of whether the roots of their perspective were Puritan or utilitarian. Similarly, Vattemare touched on the transcendentalist emphasis on the active oversoul and the achievement of self-reliance over the European muses. The idea that America raised the hope and enthusiasm of the rest of the world reinforced and ennobled these perspectives.[32]

All too soon after its establishment, Vattemare's system of exchange began to break down. Many states grew dissatisfied with the materials they received, with respect both to quality and quantity. Vattemare eagerly asserted this further underscored his conviction that a permanent agency in Paris (with himself as Director) was necessary. This did not occur. One critic characterized Vattemare's project as "somewhat visionary."[33] The Smithsonian Institution began its own international exchange in 1851. It made explicit that its system had no linkage to Vattemare's, and it was not exempt from customs duties until 1872, a price it was apparently willing to pay. In August, 1852 John S. Meehan, Librarian of Congress, stopped accepting materials from Vattemare. Vattemare kept sending boxes, however, and Meehan ordered them left unopened.[34] Massachusetts officially cut all ties with Vattemare in May, 1855.[35] Other states followed. Though clearly not fully reading the lessons at hand, Vattemare himself noted this possibility of breakdown, and it gave him pause. Upon completing his second trip to the United States he wrote to Congress:

> I bear away one source of anxiety—a fear of the permanence of that system and those relations I have been so long laboring to establish. If left to the uncertainty and charge ever incident to political affairs, no reasonable hope could be entertained of their permanent establishment.[36]

Vattemare's system fell apart due to logistical hurdles. But as Vattemare feared, America itself had produced no unified culture acceptable to all. Indeed it was breaking apart more fundamentally and tragically than was Vattemare's little experiment. Bases for unity, cultural or otherwise, did exist and could have been strengthened. Official commitment and leadership could have accentuated and facilitated this, but its pursuit entailed grave political risks none were willing to take. The political forces of sectionalism and the ideology of minimal government continued to overwhelm. Back in Europe, furthermore, Vattemare's system died with the Crimean War.

The neglect stemming from a lack of a central culture, and from conflicts between rival political factions' spilling onto spheres of culture, further revealed itself in the late 1850's when artists attempted to systematize the artistic work in the interior of the Capitol building. A report and petition bearing 129 signators, all American artists, including Albert Bierstadt, Rembrandt Peale, George Inness and Thomas Sully, came before Congress on March 3, 1859. In it the petitioners criticized the haphazard planning and esthetically eclectic nature of the art work that had been completed in the Capitol up to that point. Foreign styles and artists presented an odd assortment of styles. The petitioners held that more careful planning of the decoration of the Capitol was needed through a standing Commission which would not only coordinate matters more smoothly but promote American styles and talent.

> Let American artist, then, feel the sustaining hand of their government through the intelligent management of an Art Commission .... The result will vindicate the ability of American artists to compete with any. ... The erection and embellishment of the nation's Capitol affords the opportunity for Congress to encourage *American* art and to develop *American* genius... .[emphasis theirs] At the risk of unfriendly criticism, this committee ventures the suggestion that the field of competition could be confined to citizens of the United States, because art, to be living, must be projected from the life of a people.[37]

Congress had approved the creation of a National Art Commission in 1858 and in May, 1859 President James Buchanan named sculptor Henry K. Brown of Washington and painters James R. Lambdin of Philadelphia and John F. Kensett of New York to staff it.[38]

The Commission criticized the non-American themes employed in much of the Capitol's paintings, frescos, and statuary. Their more "American" plan, however, cost $166,900. Further costs were expected to approach $400,000. Congress balked at placing such funds into the hands of the Commission.[39] The Architects and Mechanics Journal also published a commentary, protesting perhaps jealously that no architects were placed on the Commission and that the Commission's nationalistic perspective was too narrow.[40] Congressman John Petit of Indiana further asserted "there is no occasion . . . for creating a commission to sit perpetually at a large expense."[41] It would be many decades before Congress, or the American people in general, would accept the idea of the legitimacy of standing commissions in government. The fear of centralized power subsumed the sensibilities of most, and the pre-Civil War climate of fear between various factions exacerbated this.

Notes

1. Alexis de Tocqueville, *Democracy in America*, The Henry Reeve Text. (New York: Vintage Books, 1945), Volume II, Book I, ch. 3, p. 18.

2. Henry Adams, *History of the United States* (New York, 1961), vol. I, pp. 30-31; Charles Dickens, *American Notes for General Circulation* (London, [1842] 1850), p. 81; see also James Sterling Young, *The Washington Community*, p. 13.

3. Charles Francis Adams, *The Memoirs of John Quincy Adams Comprising Portions of His Diary from 1795 to 1848* (Philadelphia, 1875-76), Vol. VII, pp. 62-3.

4. J.Q. Adams, Inaugural Address, see Samuel Flagg Bemis, *John Quincy Adams and the Founding of American Foreign Policy*, (First Edition), (New York: A.A. Knopf, 1949), pp. 55-91.

5. *Annals of Congress*, 19th Congress, 1st Session, December 13, 1825, p. 802.

6. *Annals of Congress,* vol. 30, Washington: Gales and Seaton, 1854, 14th Congress, 2d Session, pp. 762-64.

7. *Gales and Seaton's Register of Debates in Congress*, Washington: 1854, Vol. 47, part 1, 20th Congress, 1st Session, January 8-9, 1828, pp. 930-52. See also Irma B. Jaffe, *John Trumbull: Patriot Artist of the Revolution*, Boston: New York Graphic Society, 1975, pp. 259-60.

8. Ibid., p. 948.

9. Charles Lanman, "Our National Paintings," The Crayon, February 28, 1855, p. 137.

10. House Miscellaneous Document no. 496, 16th Congress, second session, American State Papers, volume 38.

11. Gales and Seaton's Register, vol. 47, 20th Congress 1st Session, January 9, 1828, IV, pt. 1, p. 942; United States Senate, Register of Debates, 18th Congress, 2d session, February 18, 1825, I, pp. 624-25.

12. John Trumbull letters to Charles Wilkes and "to" John Randolph, January 12 and 13, 1828, Yale University; and Irma Jaffe, *John Trumbull*, pp. 260-61.

13. Charles Sumner, "The Scholar, The Jurist, The Artist, The Philanthropist," (Boston, 1846), p. 45, quoted in Niel Harris, *The Artist in America*, New York, G. Braziller, 1966, p. 85.

14. U.S. Senate, *Register of Debates*, 18th Congress, 2d Session, February 18, 1825, I, p. 625; Irma B. Jaffe, *John Trumbull*, p. 9; Henry Tuckerman, *Book of the Artists*, New York, 1867, p. 85.

15. see George Fredrickson, *The Inner Civil War, Northern Intellectuals and the Crisis of the Union* (New York: Harper and Row, 1965), *passim*.

16. Senate Document no. 311, 26th Congress, 1st Session, March 24, 1840, Serial Set. 359.

17. House Document no. 229, 22d Congress, 1st Session, May 7, 1832, serial set 220; Senate Document, no. 424, 29th Congress, 1st Session, July 9, 1846, serial set 477; House Ex. Document no. 36, 36th Congress, 1st Session, March 5, 1860, serial set 1048; House Ex. Document no. 43, 36th Congress, 1st Session, April 4, 1860, serial set 1048; House Report no. 2514, 24th Congress, Second Session.

18. Nathalia Wright, Horatio Greenough, *The First American Sculptor* (Philadelphia: University of Pennsylvania Press, 1963), pp. 117-160; and Wright, ed., *Letters of Horatio Greenough, American Sculptor* (Madison: University of Wisconsin Press, 1972), *passim.*

19. W.J. Rhees, ed., *The Smithsonian Institution: Documents Relative to its Origin and History* (Smithsonian Institution: Miscellaneous Collections, XVII, Washington DC, 1879), vol. I. p. 140.

20. Ibid., pp. 163-181.

21. Geoffrey Theodore Hellman, *The Smithsonian Octopus on the Mall*, Philadelphia: Lippincott, 1967; Munro MacCloskey, *Our National Attic*, New York: R. Rosen Press, 1968; Paul Henry Oehser, *The Smithsonian Institution*, New York: Praeger, 1970; Charlotte L. Sclar, *The Smithsonian*, Jefferson, N.C.: McFarland and Co., 1985; Mark Twain, *Innocents Abroad* (New York: Harper and Brothers, [1869] 1911), p. 11.

22. Memorial of Alexandre Vattemare to the Senate and House of the United States, House Document #50, 26th Congress, 1st Session, December 10, 1839.

23. J.L. Dargent, Alexandre Vattemare, Artiste, Promoteur des Exchanges Internationaux de Publications, Tunis, Bruxelles, 1976, pp. 185-87.

24. Letters of Vattemare, January 1 to April 30, 1844, Archives of the Smithsonian; see also J.L. Dargent, *Alexandre Vattemare*, p. 156 and Elisabeth Revai, *Alexandre Vattemare trait d'Union Entre Deux Mondes*, Montreal: Les Editions Bellarmin, 1975, p. 52.

25. Joint Committee on the Library Report, Senate Document 521, June 5, 1840, 26th Congress, 1st Session.

26. House Report 539 and Senate Report 144, 28th Congress, 1st Session, January 15-25, 1844.

27. Senate Miscellaneous Documents no. 46, 30th Congress, First Session, serial sets 511 and 126, 31st Congress, First Session, serial set 563; Senate Documents nos. 559 and 521, 26th Congress, First Session, serial set 360; House Document no. 50, 26th Congress, First Session, serial set 364; and House Reports no. 586, 26th Congress, First Session, serial set 372 and no. 590, 30th Congress, First Session, serial set 526.

28. House Report 590, Ibid.

29. quoted in Dargent, *Alexandre Vattemare*, p. 184.

30. Alexis de Tocqueville, *Democracy in America*, Michel Chevalier, *Society, Manners, and Politics in the United States*, New York, (1839), A.M. Kelly, 1966.

31. *Southern Literary Messenger*, vol. 7, November, 1841, p. 783.

32. House Document no. 50, 26th Congress, First Session, serial set 364.

33. George Livermore, "Public Libraries," *North American Review*, vol. 71, July, 1850, p. 219.

34. Letters of Alexandre Vattemare, Boston Public Library.

35. Massachusetts State Library, *Catalogue of State Library*, Boston: William White, 1858, pp. XIV-XVI.

36. Senate Miscellaneous Document no. 126, 31st Congress, First Session, serial set 563.

37. House Report #198, 35th Congress, 2d Session, March 3, 1859, pp. 4-5.

38. Order of the President, May 18, 1859, Archives of the Office of the Architect of the Capitol, Washington.

39. *Documentary History of the Capitol*, House Proceedings, June 15, 1860, pp. 773-74.

40. *Architects' and Mechanics' Journal*, New York, April 7, 1860, p. 5.

41 *Documentary History of the Capitol*, p. 774.

Post-Civil War and Late Nineteenth
Century Torpor

With the coming of the Civil War, Congressional interest in support for the arts disappeared. The war needs enabled Lincoln to expand areas of government sponsored learning in the sciences. Here he expanded existing services in military, engineering, geographic and geological sectors, and he created a National Academy of Sciences. The impetus was obviously for the war effort, not for learning as an end in itself, and scientific work in the military declined precipitously after the war.[1] No evidence exists of any such efforts in the Confederacy. Southern leaders had been noticeably reticent on the subject of the arts during the ante-bellum years. They seemed to fear most any outside intrusion. Southern states were far less involved in Vattemare's work than were those of the Midwest and North, and Calhoun had argued that the government ought outright reject the legacy of James Smithson.

At the same time, some cosmopolitan/vernacular tensions appear to have been less pronounced or at least of differing form in the South. True, the benign neglect of the Louisiana Cajuns and the hillfolk of East Tennessee and the unbenign non-neglect of slaves counter an image of Southern homogeneity. And conflicts certainly existed between back-country South Carolina farmers and well-to-do Charlestonians. But a solidarity between classes existed to a greater degree than in the industrializing areas of the North, revealed, for example, in poor farmers' willingness to take up arms during slave rebellions, sacrificing without compensation time and labor otherwise spent to enhance their own livelihood. While the bases of such "ole' boy" solidarity were anything but laudable in themselves, the cultural unity to which they contributed among upper and lower ends of society existed to a high degree. The examples they set and their potential influence on other regions vanished with the war. Their reemergence in national and international letters would not come until well into the twentieth century with writers like William Faulkner and Robert Penn Warren.

The cultivated/vernacular, upper class/lower class division in American arts became most severe in the decades after the Civil War. The American artistic elite consciously turned away from its vernacular roots, seeking identity and refuge in the traditions of Europe. Meanwhile, the vernacular remained highly, often defiantly local, untouched by the technical erudition of polished Eastern contemporaries. Most illustrative here is the simultaneous flourishing of such markedly contrasting writers as Henry James and Mark Twain, of such painters as John Singer Sargent and Grandma Moses, and of composers like John Knowles Paine and Henry Clay Work. Further, older luminaries like Emerson and Longfellow, who had earlier extolled cultural unity and sought wide social breadth among their audiences, lived into the 1880s but in their last decades had far less to say to their country than they had had before the war. William Dean Howells grasped this phenomenon when he warned: "When the mass of common men have been afraid of their own simplicity, naturalness and honesty to the appreciation of the beautiful, they . . . cast about for the instruction of someone who professed to know better and who browbeat wholesome commonsense into self-distrust that ends in sophistication."[2]

Except for Walt Whitman and Thomas Eakins, few Americans could or sought to speak to or for the farmer and the industrialist. To the common laborer the arts were pure addenda. Business leaders who supported the arts generally did so as a social duty, but regarded artistic work unbefitting bright ambitious men. George Templeton Strong, for example, lawyer, philanthropist, and founder of the U.S. Sanitary Commission, was an ardent music lover and a substantive music critic. But when his son decided to become a composer, Strong disowned him completely.[3] Since the time of the founding fathers, the leadership classes had come to regard esthetics' role in a more narrow, mechanical fashion, and the esthetes rationalized their suffusion from an indifferent public that in turn saw no vitality in elite gentility.[4]

Conceivably government could have helped to bridge gaps between the cultivated and vernacular spheres of culture. The heritage of the war and the Republican orthodoxy which followed, however, apotheosized the marketplace and left all genres of culture to its whims. Elite arts here were victors' spoils.[5] Any bridging of class gaps via government sponsored culture was no more possible than meaningful economic reform in the Gilded Age. If anything the government stood in the way of the arts. In 1883, for example, Congress passed a tariff of thirty percent on imported art. This did not foster native art as much as it removed cultivated finery from popular accessibility. Attempts to remove these duties in 1884, 1886 and 1890 all failed.[6]

Congress considered several suggestions which would have prompted more affirmative national art policies. But it summarily rejected them. On February 25, 1873 a petition bearing 491 signators came before the House Committee on Labor. It made two requests. The first called for $1 million to be allotted for a National School of Art. The School was to be under Congressional control, with each member of the House to appoint one student per year from his district, copying the appointment system of West Point. Secondly, the petition asked for a quadrennial contest in American art. Submissions would become the property of the government, thus building the collection of the National Gallery at no cost. The cash prizes of $50,000 for the gold and silver medalists and $30,000 for the bronze would guarantee a sizable number of entries. This, and the idea of a National Art School, sought greater democratic involvement in the nation's artistic development. It harkened to Jefferson's idea of "raking the rubbish" for talent. The supporters sought to get around the old constraints of regional suspicion and fear of elitism. By this point, however, the content of the arguments against official support for the arts had been eclipsed by a habit of summary opposition. Neither initiative passed out of committee. They lay utterly beyond the pale of political realities.[7]

Just as tariffs involved government activism despite the rhetoric of laissez faire, so were the existence of a military academy and the failure to create a national school of art expressions of government policy that mouthed Jeffersonian platitudes but followed them selectively. Some proponents of a more active government saw the contradiction in such behavior and sought a more consistent set of policies. Supporters of the arts bills like Henry and Brooks Adams found themselves in the same position as their grandfather. Their ideas were philosophically consistent, their desires often humanistic and noble. But their opponents blithely ignored them.

Beyond the anti-intellectualism of the opposition, the unwillingness of many leaders to support the arts stemmed from a continuing sense of

American exceptionalism. If European nations did something, Americans should not, for Americans were different and better. The support of the arts in Europe had roots in key components of Europe's intellectual heritage— the Catholic Church, feudal land systems, monarchies. America had none of these. Indeed American intellectual traditions ran explicitly counter to them.

Cutting against such historical traditions placed an individual grossly out of step with the rest of the political body. No one more clearly illustrated this than Henry Adams. In his views on politics, science, and culture, Adams was a lonely traveller. He saw his country cruelly bypass all for which he stood. And as he subsequently examined the history of human initiative, he increasingly saw futility in it and suffused himself in contemplation of the distant past, in European affairs, and in pessimism. Nothing could have better reflected the wide gulf of sensibility that yawned between the average American official and Henry Adams and his friends than did a second effort by the Adams brothers and others to procure funding for an American conservatory of music and art— in Paris. They believed that the technical erudition necessary for any artist could only be gained in Europe. Not surprisingly, the House Committee on the Library of Congress never even discussed the proposal.[8] What must have gone through Adams's mind as he labored over such a proposal which he knew would fail strikes at the heart of his sad spirit.

While unsuccessful in their initiatives for either a national art contest or a national arts academy, arts minded genteel reformers had some success in supporting art training in primary and secondary education. Like Civil Service reform, the push for art training came from a combination of old-line elite Americans and new middle class German immigrants, accustomed to such programs in Europe and desirous of resurrecting them in their new homeland. Successes here came largely in states in the Northeast and Midwest with significant numbers of old elites and new Germans. Louisiana was the only Southern state to be active here as well.[9]

The Federal government's disdain for the arts continued even while the public flocked to museums and to touring exhibits. The Arts Building of the Philadelphia Centennial Exhibition drew large crowds.[10] Critics pointed out that countries like France reaped financial benefits from support for the arts. Students and tourists went there, many Americans among them, and French artist's works commanded high prices to some degree because of their national pedigree. Americans, the argument went, should strive to keep their artists at home. It would be better for the artists and for the public, culturally, spiritually, and economically. One prominent supporter of the arts in San Francisco testified before Congress:

> When French newspapers published the fact that a bill had been offered in the U.S. Senate to establish an American conservatory in Paris, all Paris smiled, and Yankee smartness dropped in the scales.

Money for the arts, he argued, is best spent at home. It is also better for the artist; otherwise:

> Your young man will adopt French ways so he won't be overcharged as an American. So he will wear baggy pants, a big black tie, and a broad brim black felt hat. He'll let his hair grow long and wear a scraggy beard ... attend balls and fetes, smoke cigarettes, and devote most of his time to some pretty little French shopgirl. He will be ashamed to come home, and his family will be ashamed to have him.[11]

Listeners may have been amused by such testimony, but it did not seem to move anyone with any authority. Further, problems existed with the argument of cost effectiveness. First, if the French had indeed cornered the art "market," others following suit could as readily fail as succeed. John D. Rockefeller was making millions in oil, but others who entered the business hardly flourished. Second, in France officialdom in the arts through the *Academie* had created problems of recognition and non-recognition over hotly debated points of esthetics. In painting, for example, Eugene Delacroix, the greatest French painter of the Romantic era, never held official recognition from the *Academie*, as his Romantic esthetic clashed with the official Classical line of Ingres. A freer, American model may have been more just to a Delacroix.

Anti-foreign sentiment did prompt government initiatives for a National Gallery of Art, a National Institute of Arts and Letters, and a National Conservatory of Music and for the purchase of the Corcoran Gallery. Support for the first three measures amounted largely to the granting of the official "National" status to privately endowed enterprises. The leaders of the National Institute, later integrated with the American Academy of Arts and Letters in New York, sought and received a federal charter but neither desired nor garnered any public funds. Supporters for the Music Conservatory argued that since American students in the arts spent $2.4 million in Europe every month (or $75 million every three years), and the Conservatory would cost but one million a year, the effort would be cost effective for the nation. American women would also be protected from the beguiling traps of a European manager who, according to one testimony, "demand much of her womanly considerations before he will consider her." Proponents wanted four conservatories—in Washington, in the New York/Boston area, in Chicago, and in San Francisco—with the hope of culling regional talent and avoiding the rise of largely traditional elites. Congress was not fully moved, and granted official sanction but minimal funds. The result was the famous National Conservatory in New York, whose first Director was Antonin Dvorak.[12]

Although traditional fine arts received little official support in nineteenth-century America, other "arts" fared better. The industrial arts, for example, though obscure to the esthete then as now, was an area in which Americans excelled in the nineteenth century, due in part to the training in state and municipally funded schools. It stands as an exception to the apparent artistic torpor of nineteenth-century America, though one which accentuated culture/class divisions: "Nowhere better [than the industrial arts] can we see the fruits of that tradition which had dedicated itself to persuading the Americans that they were a 'raw and noisy and obtrusive people.'"[13] Historians and journalists have pointed out America's deficiency in scientific research during these years, suggesting that the country was indifferent to pure science. Government support was minimal. The National Academy of Science, like the National Conservatory of Music, had official sanction with little funding. Such American scientific successes as Josiah Willard Gibbs' pioneering work in physical chemistry went virtually unnoticed in its day. While this argument has merit, it is incomplete, for American scientists were among the world leaders in such fields as geology, geography, and agronomy, and there the government, through the Smithsonian, was active. While such fields may not command the status of chemistry and physics, it is difficult to justify judgments of them as innately inferior. Similarly, industrial art holds less status than landscape painting, but the distinction is ultimately arbitrary.[14]

Generally in science the sense of linearity in its evolution and its practical payoffs made justifications easier in Congress. Congressmen who would intone high principles of minimal government and laissez-faire would readily accept funding of science. Within the arts, the government did sponsor the erection of monuments and statues, generally in commemoration of the Civil War. And portraits of various heroes were commissioned for various Federal Halls. Architecture was another art in which Americans began to assert prominence by the late nineteenth century, and the government showed some activity here too. Given the scale of the nation's growth, the need for architects was obvious. This made difficult arguments against official involvement; if the private sector could not generate a sufficient supply, foreign sources would have to be tapped. Additionally, of course, every time the government constructed a new building, an architect had to be hired. An esthetically numb Congressman could be swayed here by financial as well as by nationalistic arguments. As in other areas of political arenas, the growing complexity of industrial life was eclipsing the rhetoric of laissez faire.

Within the purely esthetic bounds of the arts, certain arguments began to erode prejudice against official support. They centered on sculpture, monument and statue design. Government reporters to various international expositions in late nineteenth-century Europe took pains to compare various genres of American art to those of the Continent, always regretfully noting America's shortcomings.[15] Such statements generally had no impact on Congressmen and others who saw this as a national strength. But some statements about America's "sacred" art struck a responsive chord. Rush Hawkins, Commissioner to the Paris Exposition of 1887, reported to the House that to learned viewers the Lincoln Statue in Springfield, Illinois when compared to the monuments of Europe, was "a commonplace pile . . . ostentatiously weak in nearly every respect . . . a curious pile devoid of intended significance or artistic expression." Of the Gettysburg battlefield, Hawkins continued:

> Let us hope that the sacred associations surrounding attempts at appropriate commemorative monuments will in the future prevent the motive being mistaken for one of caricature and that the lofty desire to justly honor noble deeds which was the primary cause of these violations of good taste, may be accepted as a mitigating excuse for their existence.[16]

Criticism similar in tone had often been directed at the ostentation of nineteenth-century Fifth Avenue or of Newport, Rhode Island. This held no significance beyond a small circle of critics. But reference to Abraham Lincoln and the Battle of Gettysburg was different. Here was a genuine point of national honor. The widespread desire to honor and respect such points of national pride and reverence compelled a reckoning with esthetic precepts. Even the most outwardly ambivalent could readily see how esthetics served noble purposes here.

Notes

1. A. Hunter DuPrée, *Science in the Federal Government, A History of Policies and Activities to 1940* (Harvard, 1957), chapters 7 and 9.

2. Perry Miller, *The Transcendentalists, Their Prose and Poetry*, (Garden City, New York: Doubleday, 1957) chapter; and John Kowenhoven, *Made in America: The Arts in Modern Civilization* (New York: Octagon Books, 1975), p. 117.

3. Vera Brodsky Lawrence, *Strong on Music*, (Vol. I) New York: Oxford University Press, 1987, *passim.*

4. John Tomsich, *The Genteel Endeavor* (Palo Alto: Stanford University Press, 1971).

5. George Frederickson, *The Inner Civil War*, and Peter Dobkin Hall, *The Organization of American Culture, 1700-1900: Private Institutions, Elites, and the Origins of American Nationality* (New York: NYU Press, 1982), Chapters 11 and 12.

6. House Document no. 111, 48th Congress, First Session, Serial Set 2206; Senate misc. doc. 28, 48th Congress, 1st Session, Serial Set 2171; Senate misc. doc. 22, 49th Congress, 1st Session, Serial Set 2342; Senate ex. doc. 91, 51st Congress, First Session, Serial Set 2686.

7. Senate Miscellaneous Document no. 89, 42d Congress, 3d Session, serial set 1546.

8. Senate Document no. 359, 57th Congress, First Session, serial set 4245.

9. Senate ex. document 209, 46th Congress, 2d Session, Serial Sets 1888 and 1889-1, 2, and 3, pp. 660-689.

10. Ibid., Serial Set 1888, p. xxxvi.

11. Senate Document 359, 57th Congress, 1st Session, Serial Set 4245.

12. Senate Report 570, 53d Congress, 2d Session, Serial Set 3192; House Report 3402, 51st Congress, 2d Session, Serial Set 2885; Senate Doc. 359, 57th Congress, First Session, Serial Set 4245; on the Corcoran Gallery: Senate Report no. 137, 49th Congress, First Session, Serial Set 2358; House Report no. 3049, 49th Congress, First Session, Serial Set 2444; Senate Report no. 960, 54th Congress, First Session, Serial Set 3366.

13. John Kouwenhoven, *Made In America, The Arts in Modern Civilization* (New York: Octagon Books, 1975), pp. 113-17.

14. Hunter Dupree, *Science in the Federal Government*, chapters 8 and 10; John Kouwenhoven, *Made in America, passim*; Richard Hofstadter, *Anti-Intellectualism in American Life*, New York: Knopf, 1963, p. 25-6; on the Industrial Arts, Senate ex. document 209, 46th Congress, 2d Session, Serial Set 1888; Senate Report 927, 50th Congress, 1st Session, Serial Set 2523.

15. House Misc. Documents, 40th Congress, 2d Session, Serial Sets 1351, 1352, 1353; House ex. Doc. 42, 46th Congress, 3d Session, Serial Set 1971; House ex. Doc. 410, 51st Congress, 1st Session, Serial Set 2754; Senate

Document 232, 56th Congress, 2d Session, Serial Sets 4056 and 4057.

16. House ex. doc. 410, 51st Congress, 1st Session, Serial Set 2754, p. 4.

The Beginnings of Activism

In the 1890s numerous writers began to write of the nation "coming of age." Given the spectre of entering into a new century, writers, editors, politicians, and many others asserted it was time for the United States to display its social and cultural maturity. A nation capable of standing as an equal among the world's powers ought to have more than a high GNP. There were numerous forms of activity through which this maturity could be displayed: a colonial empire, a strong navy, a more aggressive foreign policy, lower tariffs, improved conditions for the poor, cleaner and more efficient governments, more beautiful cities and municipalities, and achievement in the arts and letters. Actions along these many lines often worked at cross purposes, but one common theme involved the need for more active government. While the shibboleths of laissez faire and social Darwinism had been minimizing government action, these constraints appeared platitudinous amidst the economic depression of the 90s and as the complexity of a modern world compelled a search for more sophisticated, overt guidance of human affairs.

The 1893 Chicago World's Fair and the resulting "City Beautiful" movement pricked the consciousness of many Americans. A Public Arts League was formed by members of the American Institute of Architects and of Washington's Cosmos Club. Its members thought that Washington needed beautification and not merely through scattered, uncoordinated action but through careful long term planning. Like those sensitive to the impugning of Lincoln and Gettysburg, Washingtonians wished their city to stand with Paris and London and not as an embarrassment. With its extreme summer heat and humidity, malaria, TB, yellow fever, and dearth of social life, late nineteenth-century Washington was hardly a garden spot. Indeed many European diplomats regarded it as a hardship post. The Architects' Institute and the Cosmos Club held that a permanent, official body of experts in art, architecture, landscape design, and sculpture ought oversee a program to beautify Washington with parks, monuments, and general urban planning. In 1897 they sought legislation to establish such a body with a staff of five: two Presidential appointees and the Presidents of the American Institute of Architects, the National Academy of Design, and the National Sculpture Society. The bill failed, principally because of Congressional objections to the latter three members being appointed by neither the President nor Congress and to the commission's power being anything more than advisory.

Though this effort did not succeed, there emerged a growing sense that scientific expertise could and should be marshalled to serve an end that was both esthetic and ethical in nature. In 1899 and 1900 momentum gathered along these lines with the approach of the city's 100th anniversary. President McKinley called for Washington's centennial to be a notable event, and newspapers in New York, Philadelphia, Indianapolis, Cincinnati, Charleston, and of course Washington all wrote editorials calling for the beautification of the capital in view of the anniversary.[1]

In 1900 the American Institute of Architects held its convention in Washington as part of the celebration. There a number of papers argued for beautification. In 1901 the Institute's suggestions led the Senate in 1901 to create a Park Commission (known since as the MacMillan Commission, after its chairman, Senator James MacMillan of Michigan). The Commission's membership included Daniel Burnham, the leader of Chicago's architectural efflorescence, landscape architect Frederick Law Olmsted, Jr., architect Charles McKim, and sculptor Augustus St. Gaudens.

The MacMillan Commission developed plans for the physical reorganization of Washington, its members travelling to London, Paris, Rome, Vienna, Venice, and Budapest to inspect park and public building design. They reported to Congress at the end of 1901, recommending a coordinated park system. Drawing from the District's original L'Enfant Plan of 1791, they paid particular attention to the beautification of the Capitol Mall, recommending an extension of the Mall from the Capitol past the Washington Monument to the Potomac River, with a new memorial to Lincoln to be built at the river end. The Pennsylvania Railroad owned tracks on the site of the proposed mall. One of

Burnham's chief accomplishment during his Commission's year of work was to persuade the Railroad's President Alexander J. Cassatt to remove the tracks. The Commission disbanded within a year, leaving many of its plans in abeyance. But the perspective of various Washington officials in regard to the role of esthetic considerations in public policy was beginning to shift.

Activities like the City Beautiful movement of the turn of the century reflected an increasing readiness to see government take an active role in esthetic enterprises. With this grew a greater need and respect for experts in various artistic and intellectual fields. Robert LaFollette's Wisconsin experiment was the best known state level change in the status of the expert and intellectual in government. On the national level, Theodore Roosevelt made a comparable contribution, although ambiguities crop up in any assessment of his work. Many reforms had been enacted before Roosevelt, and many were passed in spite of him. But his activist image signaled a new time when the old official ideal of minimal, passive government appeared dead. Roosevelt was the first President since John Quincy Adams to take up such an outwardly activist perspective and give lip service to as well as take at least some concrete action in support of the arts and the life of creativity. He brought to Washington a number of intellectuals and artists for service and advice, and made at least a good show of his enjoyment of intellectual repartee.[2] Historians have discussed Roosevelt's ambivalence with regard to intellect, how he could turn on intellectuals, once regarded as friends, over trivial matters, how he was ultimately unsystematic in most of his endeavors, how he tied his vision of a good society to his amorphous notion of "good character."[3]

At the very end of his Presidency, Roosevelt nudged forward the work of the defunct MacMillan Commission. On January 18, 1909, but six weeks before leaving office, the lame duck President responded to an appeal from the American Institute of Architects and issued an Executive Order creating a Council on the Fine Arts. The thirty-member Council was to advise on structural, design, and esthetic issues regarding public buildings, bridges, parks, sculptures and paintings. The Council met but once under Roosevelt, a month before Taft was to take office. Its members approved the MacMillan Commission's recommendations for a Mall and a Lincoln Memorial.

Taft favored the concept of an Art Commission. Illustrative of his legalistic manner, however, he abolished the Commission Roosevelt had created, holding that an act of Congress and not an Executive Order was the proper basis for establishment. Taft supported legislation for the formation of an official Federal Commission of Fine Arts. New York Senator Elihu Root sponsored the act of incorporation in 1910.

Earlier that year an Institute of Arts and Letters had been proposed to Congress. This National Institute was to have 250 members. The membership was impressive, including politicians Roosevelt, Henry Cabot Lodge, and Woodrow Wilson, writers Henry and Brooks Adams, William Dean Howells, Henry James, Mark Twain, and Finley Peter Dunne, philosophers Josiah Royce and George Santyana, painters John Singer Sargent, Robert Henri, and Winslow Homer, and musicians Victor Herbert, Walter Damrosch, and Charles Martin Loeffler. The Joint Congressional Committee on the Library of Congress had suggested the Institute's formation. It had the responsibility of purchasing and collecting documents and works of art for the government, and felt the need for expert guidance. The Committee admitted feeling at sea when it came to passing judgments on such matters as the purchase of paintings. It was also concerned with space and organization problems facing the Library of Congress. Several Congressmen proposed that a Library annex be built. This of course compounded the need for expert advice on esthetic matters. The Committee indeed held that the annex should be planned with sensitivity to the architectural and landscape patterns of the city.

The organization, preservation, purchasing and housing of works of art all required expert advice and judgment. If Congress was serious about these historical, artistic, and architectural matters, the Committee argued, then it should seek expert assistance. The House deadlocked eighty-three to eighty-three in its vote on the Institute, so the bill did not pass. But the closeness of the vote indicated the degree to which sensibilities in Washington had changed.

Twice before Congress had moved along these lines. In 1892 the Senate Committee on Washington called for an advisory "academy" on purchases and placements as part of a bill to establish an art gallery in the District. Since the academy's members would donate their services gratis, the move required no funding and met no objection. In 1896 the House Committee on the Library of Congress similarly authorized a voluntary five-person committee to oversee collections and screen purchases.[4] When Root's more broadly ranging Fine Arts Council came before Congress in 1910, some of the suggestions of these forerunners would engender ridicule from Council opponents.

The large Institute discussed in early 1910 was apparently too broad in membership and scope to win acceptance. But a small advisory council, as had existed in the 1890's and under Roosevelt, was more appropriate. The Commission that Root proposed would advise on artistic purchases and on the beautification of Washington. Its annual budget would be only $10,000. Still, objections arose. Many expressed concern over the "advisory" nature of the Council. Senator Weldon Heyburn of Idaho wanted a greater level of Congressional oversight over the Council expressly written into the enabling legislation. Congressman John Fitzgerald of New York also called for more oversight, since "some of our Presidents have not been noted for their particularly ideal artistic taste." Both amending efforts failed.[5]

Stronger reservations arose over the Council's budget; not, surprisingly, because it was too large but too small. One of Root's arguments, echoing the successful efforts of the 1890s, was that the Council would do its work with minimal cost to the taxpayer. No costs would exist beyond those of administration and logistics, the Council members donating their services out of public spirit. Senator Heyburn warned that biases would result from the class perspective of "gentlemen of leisure:"[6]

> You shut out by the terms of this bill all of that class of artists who have from the very earliest pages of history been recorded as poor and unable to contribute without compensation for such services. Rembrandt could not have reached Washington from Baltimore.[7]

Earlier in the 1910 session and again in 1913 the same criticism was raised against the ill-fated Academy. Heyburn proposed each member be paid $3000 per year, so the membership pool could extend beyond rich gentlemen. Root strongly disagreed with this "mere salary basis," and Heyburn's amendment failed. The whole debate here was a microcosm of the strange bedfellows which early twentieth-century reform prompted. Conservatives opposing government activism joined with radicals and Populists who wanted full, systematic changes and stood against Progressive liberals whose efforts appeared half-way and elitist.[8]

Distrustful of the narrow range of sensibilities in a commission of gentlemen of leisure, critics also worried that all advisors would hail from the Northeast. This geographical concern had long been on the minds of critics of officialdom in the arts. Since opposition was waning, it came with greater specificity. Speaking in favor of the Commission, Congressman Henry A. Cooper of Wisconsin, cited the views of an artist:

Now I read that an artist—I do not know whether he was an artist, but at any rate he was from Boston.

Mr. James R. Mann [of Illinois, interrupting]: The same thing (laughter).[9]

The old Jacksonian image persisted of the Northeast harboring those capable only of life's impracticalities. Indeed during the debate when some pro-Commission Congressmen pointed out that New York City supported such a body, Congressmen William W. Campbell of Ohio snorted: "I have never advised anywhere that New York City's example be followed in government."[10] New York, furthermore, had engaged in such extravagances as arts councils and a large education system and accumulated a huge debt. Many Congressmen always put the ledger above the spirit.

Closely related to Congressman James Mann's image of the rich Northeastern artist, incapable of life's real chores, was the suggestion that artists themselves might not be the best judges or advisors. Senator Elmer Burkett of Nebraska snarled:

There has always been a coterie of so-called artists—I will withdraw the term "so called," because I think they are artists, at least nominally—but they have been trying to get away from Congress the work of beautifying this District. ... Some of them got their work in ... a few years ago, and I have not heard a man speak of the result who did not say their achievement ... has been more or less a botch.[11]

Several Congressmen brought up the generally agreed upon ugliness of the Barry Statue and the Grant Memorial in Washington's Botanical Gardens.[12] These results of expert advice from official committees in the 1890s hardly bode well for the new Commission. Senator Burkett added with a new form of DC provincialism that artists were in no position to beautify Washington, for they had little acquaintance with it:

There is a different history here; there are different traditions about the city ... that we must respond to, ... and it is fair to say that people here know more about how to beautify Washington in keeping with the history traditions ... than any coterie of artists ... from New York, Boston or anywhere else ... . We want their suggestions, but not their domination.[13]

The most fundamental criticism reflected the fear that the Commission would inexorably transcend its advisory status and develop autonomous power. Minnesota Congressman James Tawney saw this possibility closely related to the socially elitist artistic character of the membership. They would, he predicted, "assume to exercise functions and powers whether we authorize them or not. "They are a class of men that do not know anything about law, and respect it less when it interferes with what they believe to be the artistic line along which we should go."[14] Viewing the Commission more broadly, as part of the growing bureaucratization of the U.S. Government, Congressman Robert B. Macon of Arkansas lamented:

> This government is today burdened with commissions. It will not be long before [it] will be commission ridden and the taxable burdens the people must bear will be unendurable. ... Ah, Mr. Chairman, the commission business has run mad. ... In all of this we are apt to forget the boy who is following the plow ... or the man who is digging deep in the earth with his pick.[15]

Congressman William Campbell echoed these views. And his views apparently resonated with some colleagues and viewers when he proclaimed:

> My opposition to this bill is that it creates another commission (Applause), which in time will be converted into a bureau or department. ... For one, I have long since tired of seeing the Government of the United States gradually handed over to commissions and bureaus. (Renewed Applause).[16]

James Tawney, Robert Macon, William Campbell and many other Congressmen regarded the resort to a commission in order to counter the unresponsive, corrupt practices of government to be a mere switch of masks. Government would remain as or more unresponsive to the population at large. Corruption would be negated, but only by comparably more expensive legal administrative costs. Senator Weldon Heyburn and Congressmen Tawney and Campbell stood firmly by the principle that Congress should do its job and not delegate responsibility. Robert Macon was more extreme in his opposition. He contended that if a monument needed to be built, the people would take the initiative on their own. A commission goes about such tasks, Macon noted, in a "metallic way," while free citizens do so out of love.[17] Here lay the classic debate between the Jeffersonian ideal of government of "the people" and the Hamiltonian lean toward government by "experts." Philosophically the debate could not be resolved, then or since. But in the context of a modernizing, technological America, the Hamiltonian tended to win.

On May 17, 1910, despite this varied opposition, Congress authorized the Commission. The money involved remained minimal: $10,000 per year. The critical determinant in passage appears to have been the belief in higher wisdom of those with specific training, skills and talents. Considering the tension within Progressivism between the desire to restore the traditions of individual entrepreneurialism in economic life and of democracy in politics, and the desire to make public and private institutions work better through the incorporation of experts, the Arts Commission clearly represented the latter.

A key question in judging the Progressive character of the Arts Commission concerns whether or not its esthetic judgments varied with popular sensibilities. Thinking of the Barry and Grant monuments and of the elite backgrounds of the Commission's membership, some Congressional critics predicted such a clash. But the major works of the Commission have generally won strong popular approval. The Commission has developed or advised on over 40,000 projects. Among the more famous ones were the Lincoln and Jefferson Memorials, the Capitol Mall, the expansion and development of Rock Creek Park and of the Tidal Basin, Cherry Blossom Park, neighborhood preservation and development of Georgetown and Lafayette Square, the Kennedy Center for the Performing Arts, the Watergate Complex, and the Vietnam Memorial. Some stylistic criticism has cropped up. The Jefferson Memorial, for example, built in the late 1930s, was Washington's last serene, stately classically styled memorial of the Beaux Arts tradition. This was the preferred style of the first Commissioners. By the late 1930s critics of more modernist taste found the style pompous and academic. More recent designs, such as I.M. Pei's addition to the National Gallery of Art, sparked counter reactions from anti-modernists. As the velocity of stylistic change grows, such conflict looms increasingly unavoidable. The construction of the D.C. Metropolitan Railway system sparked some public and neighborhood conflict with the Commission, for the Commission wanted the same design for each Metro stop. Others wanted diversity. The Commission insisted and had its way.

Beyond esthetics controversies have arisen. The Watergate Complex has sparked controversy but not of an artistic sort. Neighborhood development in Georgetown and Lafayette Square has sparked the terribly complex political dilemmas involving gentrification and displacement of the poor. Some raised the question of the irreverence in the rapidity with which the memorial to Robert Taft was erected so soon after his death.

The fears that the Commission would expand its power and develop a vast bureaucracy have proven unwarranted. Few charges of arbitrariness have arisen. Including secretarial staff, only ninety-six people served on the Commission from 1910 to 1976. Rarely have more than ten sat at any one time. Money spent for administrative costs has been minimal. Indeed, in most years the Commission has done its work under budget.

The Fine Arts Commission has had considerable significance in and of itself. It has performed, and continues to perform, significant tasks for the nation and for the Capital. The Vietnam War monument gave perspective to that experience and lent solace through camaraderie to the veterans and to the next of kin, accomplishing the work of a thousand psychiatrists. The Commission provided the first permanent Federal initiatives towards any of the arts.

Notes

1. Senate Document no. 209, 56th Congress, First Session, Serial Set 3857.

2. In various letters to recognized men of letters one senses someone terribly pleased with himself yet a bit strained, perhaps sensing his having reached his limits. See, for example his correspondence with G.M. Trevelyan in Elting E. Morison, ed., *The Letters of Theodore Roosevelt*, (Harvard University Press, 1951), vols. 3 and 4, pp. 667, 706, 806, 1043, 1132, and 1173, and vols. 5 and 6, pp. 696, 785, and 1397.

3. see Hofstadter, *Anti-Intellectualism*, p. 207.

4. Senate Report 932, 52d Congress, 1st Session, Serial Set 2915, re Senate Bill 1922; House Report 2136, 54th Congress, 1st Session, Serial Set 3465.

5. *Congressional Record-House*, Volume 45, Part 2, 61st Congress, 2d Session, February 9, 1910, p. 1671 and May 3, 1910, p. 5708.

6. Ibid., May 3, 1910, p. 5707.

7. Ibid., May 2, 1910, p. 5652.

8. Ibid., May 3, 1910, p. 5705.

9. Ibid., February 9, 1910, p. 1663.

10. Ibid., p. 1662.

11. Ibid., May 3, 1910, p. 5706.

12. Ibid., February 9, 1910, pp. 1660 and 1666.

13. Ibid., May 3, 1910, p. 5706.

14. Ibid., February 9, 1910, p. 1661.

15. Ibid., p. 1665.

16. Ibid., p. 1662

17. Ibid.

A Retrospective on Government and the Arts in the Nineteenth Century

Compared to the major European governments of the nineteenth century, the American government's participation in the arts was minimal. In the nineteenth century the United States became the first powerful nation in the world to hold that the arts were best left purely in private hands. The United States had none of the deeply rooted aristocratic, monarchical or religious institutions which in Europe had traditionally accepted and systematized an officialdom in the arts. Not only did America have none of this, many of its political and cultural traditions emerged from a conscious challenge to those very habits. Though the purview of Federal power was always a subject of strong debate, the Constitution, particularly in its early interpretations, placed significant limits on Federal activism. Even leaders of the early nineteenth century like Henry Clay, contemporaneously viewed as loose constructionists, held reservations as to the legitimacy of Federal activism in various spheres or at least respectfully acknowledged the legitimacy of such reservations in others.

Many of the Founding Fathers entertained ideas about nationally sponsored programs of learning and creativity. Each of the first six Presidents considered, in various forms, the establishment of a national university. But various events and circumstances got in the way. For some like Thomas Jefferson such flights of intellectual fancy had to be reconciled with his own, and his supporters' idealization of minimal federal power. Conversely, John Quincy Adams had to confront the political reality that wary opponents held such Jeffersonian views. Adams' proposals for government aid to science, education and the arts further rallied his opponents whose sensibilities came to dominate at least the political rhetoric if not the actual ideology of early and mid nineteenth-century politics. The Jacksonian or democratic turn of American politics may have involved more a mere switch of elites in national leadership than any genuine empowerment of the common people. But the transformation here did involve a diffusion of power to a variegated, ideologically more eclectic set of competing elites, among whom any systematic unity of principles was never worth deep consideration. Within this, anti-elitism readily modulated into anti-intellectualism. The intellectual clarity and purposefulness of earlier political leaders could accommodate, or negate, as diverse a set of plans as John Quincy Adams outlined in his inaugural address. But such government by ideology gave way to less systematic patronage and rhetoric, what Tocqueville described as a society growing "more democratic, less brilliant." Thus fragmented, the politically weak spheres which won some support in pre-Jacksonian days fell victim to ambivalence as well as to opposition. They could not generate a significant voice in the new disjointed political marketplace, and such genres as the arts had to turn to private resources.

In a privatized state, gaps widened between the cultures of rich and poor, cultivated and vernacular, classical and popular, East/West, North/South, urban/rural. The potential cohesiveness from Federal involvement was gone. The political forces which had prompted the democratic or Jacksonian transformation drew rhetorical capital from such divisions and extended them. While debates in the early nineteenth century involved whether or not there should be a national university or general government sponsorship of science and the arts, subsequent generations debated such more narrow concerns as whether painters should be employed to create works for the corridors of the Capitol; whether a sculpture should have distinct status from a slab of stone with respect to tariffs; should the government accept a legacy from James Smithson, and if so should a museum be constructed in Washington? Might one region or class unduly benefit? The debates here were vehement, and the purview granted was quite narrow.

Though little ground was given, respect for the arts and for formal learning remained in the hearts of leaders as diverse as Thomas Hart Benton and Daniel Webster. When Alexandre Vattemare's program of international library exchanges between Europe, Canada and the United States came before the Senate expressions of support glowed. The program fizzled, however. Support had largely involved but words.

For the remainder of the century individuals like Henry Adams, who understood the requirements for substantive government activity in artistic and intellectual endeavors, continually found themselves on the political periphery. Some of their ideas were intriguing—a National Art School modeled upon West Point's entrance methods, allowing each Congressman to cull talent from his district; a National Art Contest with all entries becoming the government's possession, allowing the prize money in effect to pay cheaply for a build up in the National Gallery's collection. But none of the suggestions even passed out of committee onto the floor of Congress. Henry Adams and his friends anticipated this, accepting their impotence and their role as gadflies. Indeed once they sardonically proposed the government establish an American Art School in the one city they felt could give American arts a sympathetic home—Paris.

The gap of sensibility between those interested in nurturing the arts and those in political power had grown cavernous. In the first decade of the century was Jefferson; in the last was Speaker of the House Thomas Reed. For Jefferson the arts, along with all walks of intellectual life, were of interest, and command over them was essential for a thoughtful leader in a democracy, i.e., for a true statesman. To Reed a statesman was a successful politician who was dead. Indeed when the great painter John Singer Sargent presented Reed's portrait, Reed could only sniff: "all my enemies are now avenged." Reed had no feel for culture. He could see no point in it beyond decoration. His thinking could only occupy a political context. And his humor ultimately revealed a cynical depravity of spirit about art.

It is the height of pomposity, and simply wrong, to view the likes of James G. Blaine, Roscoe Conkling and Thomas Reed as intellectually inferior to the Founding Fathers. Each were of their own eras, though eras which contrasted mightily with respect to perspectives on how humans could control their own affairs. Leaders of Jefferson's day saw men best in front of events, shaping them more than being shaped by them. To achieve this the many paths of learning and creativity had to be mastered and integrated. For their grandchildren, even the brightest seemed at least a few steps behind the waves of world affairs. Rationalizing this perception, they viewed much of humanity's creation to be best dispassionately weighed in terms of political usefulness and used, and placated or ignored accordingly.

As Reed and his generation of leaders were more of than above their time, they had no grasp of the spiritual appeal in the arts which can involve the very temporal transcendence for which they had no capacity. Then as now, such people cannot be converted or changed, but their very lack of spirituality invariably leaves them eclipsed upon changes in human affairs, for they have nothing which transcends their own eras. And the generations of Roscoe Conkling, James G. Blaine, and Tom Reed hardly stand high compared with those of Washington, Jefferson, and John Quincy Adams. Indeed, Henry Adams noted this very transformation in the species of American leaders and speculated such a devolution called Darwin's Theory of Evolution into question. Such desultory character as Reed and his contemporaries exemplified serves at least as a metaphor for the quick passing of their sensibilities before the newer turn-of-the-century dynamics loosely labeled Progressivism and internationalism. Reed indeed quickly left power as America's orientation grew more international and activist in economic and political matters. These very transformations in the early twentieth century brought government into greater levels of involvement and regulation, and those in the arts and in intellectual endeavors found more sympathy and support in regard to their roles in public life.

Such varied leaders of the early twentieth century as Robert LaFollette, Theodore Roosevelt and Woodrow Wilson personally saw great value in the life of the mind, though some would have it that Roosevelt merely made a good show of such a value. Even if that was the case, Roosevelt's desire to make such a posture reveals a changed set of sensibilities he perceived among the general public in regard to the utility of intellect. Progressive leaders also recognized that in the desire to make American institutions work more efficiently or democratically, or to make these institutions and the nation more appealing to a world community in which they saw themselves playing an ever more significant role, the integration of spiritual, intellectual and artistic endeavors into public policies was necessary. A great nation had to have more than large factories. A sensitivity to charges of boorishness was keen among those leaders who favored public efforts to beautify Washington, D.C., and the resulting National Commission on the Arts became the first permanent government initiative in the realm of the arts.

The general tenor of Progressivism ended the nineteenth-century apotheosization of laissez-faire and social Darwinism. These two perspectives would form the antipodes of a series of pendulum swings in twentieth-century American politics of which public funding for the arts has been a part. After World War I the Republican ascendency, which mouthed nineteenth-century platitudes of minimal government (while actually expanding national government power in many contexts) would muffle Progressivism. In the 20s the government would take few initiatives in the realm of the arts. With the Depression activism would again swell, the New Deal WPA arts projects being the most significant initiatives in this context. The projects died during World War II, and amidst the "Had Enough" Congress of the late 40s and the Eisenhower calm of the 50s, Federal initiatives in the arts would again fall away, though many calls for action would come forth, motivated particularly by concerns about Soviet prowess in culture. In the 60s and 70s activism would reach new heights with the establishment of the National Endowments for the Arts and Humanities. Despite many general postures about minimal government, the Republicans of the 70s and 80s would never actually reverse this development, though some budget cutting would take place. Generally the twentieth century would, unlike the nineteenth, witness an increase of government involvement in the arts, though resistance would remain keen. Whether the activism has been good or bad remains a judgment for each citizen. Debates over the legitimacy of Federal presence in the arts are among the issues which when discussed intelligently go to the heart of the meaning and intent of the Constitution as well as to the elusive question of the relationship of public policy to a people's collective spirit. Such debates always engage a healthy democracy.

The New Deal and the Arts — the Early Initiatives and the Heritage of The Writers' Project

After the passage of the Commission of Fine Arts, Congress did little until the Depression in support of the arts. In 1913 another attempt failed at establishing an American Academy of Arts and Letters, similar to the National Institute proposed in 1910. Quasi-populist, anti-East Coast arguments were pronounced in the debates. The Commission was focused on organizing the planning and beautification of Washington, D.C. Anything broadly defined like a National Institute or Academy would obviously influence all regions of the country. Such French *Academie*-type centralization of cultural standards appears to have been too much beyond the norms for American leaders. Such nationalization of culture would continue to elicit opposition throughout the twentieth century.

One small successful effort in regard to arts' support came in March of 1920 when the act of 1891, creating a National Conservatory of Music, gained amendments to allow for the establishment of new branches beyond the original New York site. Through the decade of the twenties, aside from the work of the Fine Arts Commission, the government did nothing for the arts and, if anything, worked negatively, raising tariffs on imported works of art and restricting their exportation.[1]

With the onset of the Depression, the restrictive mood of many Congressmen continued. In 1936 Representative Joseph Dickstein of New Jersey proposed a bill, for example, to place quotas on the number of foreign actors, musicians, and dancers who could perform in the United States at any one time. During the Depression unemployment had affected the performing arts as adversely as any profession. In 1936, for example, 15,000 actors were on relief. Such a state made foreign actors and performers easy targets for political attacks from Congressmen and others. Discussions over complexities in the enforcement of Dickstein's bill brought it to failure. Was conductor Arturo Toscanini, for example, to be kept from performing? Supporters of the bill attempted to develop language to exclude "stars" from the proposed restrictions. This opened thorny questions of definition which legislators envisioned could not be answered by particular Immigration officers or Labor Department officials before whom such matters would appear. Sensitive to such complexities, the American Federation of Musicians, the Musicians Union, and the Motion Picture Producers Association all opposed the bill. Congressman Emanuel Celler of New York held: "You cannot treat artists in quotas as so many sacks of potatoes or bales of cotton." The House tabled the bill.[2]

Amidst the debate over the bill, critics raised the point that certain plays, dealing, for example, with English country life, required actors of certain background and accent. While such notions further contributed to the bill's tabling, the criticism illuminated the fact that various components of the arts in America remained strongly tied to European culture, the best allegedly being that which was most in step with the latest trends of the European centers. In the thirties, in a conscious challenge to this sense of inferiority, rose a desire for increased national and sectional identifiability in the arts. Not only had artists, writers, and musicians continuously taken cues from the latest developments in European capitals, but audiences had also appeared to remain wedded to the notion that European culture was somehow better. Indeed amidst shrinking profits during the depression curators, theatre managers, and symphony and opera boards tended toward the "safe" repertory of European classics, fearing anything experimental might drive away what precious, and generally conservative, clientele they had left. The cosmopolitan/vernacular division in the arts which had grown in the nineteenth century continued to suffuse elites into a holding pattern in which the haut culture of Europe provided a veneer of rooting. The division further restricted people of vernacular cultures from access to institutions that taught many of the finer points of technique. Both sides remained estranged.

By the 1930s this division manifested itself in many forms, most clearly among cosmopolitans who created in often impenetrable, avantgarde styles and among vernacularists who lacked and often eschewed knowledge of established modes of craftsmanship. In the decade of the 1930s came a softening of these lines. Though some bridges had been built before, the degree of exchange between the cultivated and the vernacular grew tremendously. Aaron Copland, predominantly an avant-garde musician in the 1920s, reflected on a desire to be more communicative:

> During the mid-'30's I began to feel an increasing dissatisfaction with the relations of the music-loving public and the living composer. ... I felt it was worth the effort to see if I couldn't say what I had to say in the simplest possible terms.[3]

At the same time Duke Ellington "made a lady out of jazz, drawing freely in his writings from the innovations of many "classical" composers, particularly Claude Debussy and Maurice Ravel. Indeed Ellington sought altogether to abandon the label "jazz," viewing it as too restrictive in regard to the sounds he sought to achieve. He preferred "American music." Many factors were at work in this confluence of previously distinct genres in the arts. Perhaps of deepest significance was the subsuming commonality of economically hard times which rendered trivial many prior points of distinction. Within this came the discovery of the beauty and nobility of the struggles of so many previously ignored and downtrodden. The government played a role here too through the programs of the New Deal and the esthetic precepts they promoted.

While the Fine Arts Commission and other earlier initiatives brought the Federal government into some positions of activism in the arts, the programs of the New Deal marked a genuine change in kind as well as degree. One salient feature of all the New Deal programs that pertained to the arts was the dimension of relief. This element distinguishes New Deal from government arts programs, then and since, for the thrust of the initiatives was not wholly, or even principally, esthetic. Yet esthetic dimensions came to the fore in public discussions over the legitimacy of the New Deal activities, discussions which echoed many previous concerns about government and the arts and which anticipated matters that have arisen in more recent times.

The economic circumstances which prompted New Deal efforts were unprecedented. The number of unemployed was staggering in all areas. In addition to general economic cycles, technological developments in the arts heightened the troubles. Talking films, for example, grew enormously in 1928 and 1929. This ended the employment of virtually all

movie theatre musicians. The ever widening popularity of radio and
phonographs, both much cheaper than concert going, further decreased
demand for live musical performances. And of course the general public expenditures on musical performances dwindled with the depression.[4] At first the government treated the artists like any of the unemployed and gave them relief. This began with the Federal Emergency
Relief Act (FERA).

The FERA's work, as its title implies, consisted of straightforward
relief for people of many professions. In regard to the arts, its significance lay in its granting of relief to writers, many of whom had been laid
off by magazines and newspapers which were folding in large numbers.
Though most of the funding involved direct relief payments, some localities began to establish writing and arts projects with the relief money.
The idea of using funds for such projects did not adhere to the idea of
basic relief. Controversies, though largely implicit at this point, fore-
shadowed many that later in the decade would come forth more fully.
Critics could have charged that such projects added codicils to the
money's availability not embodied in the original legislation. Right
wing criticism of relief preferred such projects over direct cash payments, as projects lent ethical value and direction. Some pro-relief people felt a programmatic approach would yield preferential treatment to
those who could fit esthetic standards which were independent of economic needs. A good artist, more likely better off than a less capable
colleague, would be apt to gain more, yielding less for those possibly in
greater need. So instituted, such programs could further empower the
bureaucracies of these projects' administrators and compel states and
localities to defer to power in Washington. All such points could serve
to unite the left-leaning and anti-elite critics of projects with the anti big
government critics on the right. Such conundrums would rattle about
during the New Deal work for the arts, as it would with respect to other
activities. In the early years, however, such debates remained largely
implicit. Neither the luxury nor the time for such discussions yet existed, and critics on the right and left were generally small and unorganized
minorities. Relief was desperately needed and received applause when it
came. Neither proponents nor critics of the New Deal had formulated
concepts that approached anything systematic, nor had the questions
reached the general public to any degree.

The FERA's relief projects would expand with the Civil Works
Administration (CWA). The FERA was a principal backdrop to the
CWA but not the sole one. Also important were several local efforts,

three in particular in Philadelphia, New York and Los Angeles. These local projects reinforced the pattern that held for reforms at the turn of the century involving ideas working their way up from lower government levels to the national scene. While this appears almost truistic, it does cut against the often written orthodoxy of the New Deal being so different from earlier reform movements, a Washington-centered phenomenon tied little to preceding or contemporaneous state and local initiatives.

With the CWA initiatives the inherent value of the work done began to rival the concept of relief. Projects each had an explicit focus on the artistic work at hand.[5] The surrounding political and social content of many of these artistic activities also began to take on increasing importance. With this transformation slippery problems arose involving the politicization of definitions and evaluations in artistic matters.

As the arts entered further into the political arena, many New Dealers were not the least fearful. Rather they optimistically asserted that the panorama of political and social matters at hand, from workers wages and conditions to the content and style of murals on the walls of new buildings, could all be subjected to scientifically precise management and engineering. With this perspective cultural artifacts, be they objects of art, novels, or concerts, could no longer be regarded as mere analogues of life. Like political and economic dynamics, they now held paradigmatic value in the shaping and adjusting of the society. Culture thus ceased to be the toy of the elite, irrelevant to the social mainstream. The depression had levelled many such social distinctions and closed gaps between vernacular and patrician values. The arts, like the economy, presented planners with a blank slate. Radicals welcomed such a state. Conservatives feared it, but both recognized it. The New Deal would prove unfulfilling to those who hoped for a systematic restructuring, but in the early years the hopes were not yet frustrated.

Heightening the hopes for fundamental changes in the social structure of the society was the apparent demise of much art which had previously been the domain of the wealthy. Many avant-garde idioms, consciously pursued in the twenties as trademarks of elite status, had grown disgraced, curios of a by-gone age, examples of how silly and decadent those times had been. Reactions to the art of the twenties were quite severe, to the point that much sincere work of the previous decade was tossed off with the frivolous art, revealing both guilt and anger among those formerly well-off and indulgent of abnormality. Sensitive to the sobering times around him, Richard Skinner, a sternly orthodox music

critic of the Catholic and conservative *Commonweal*, reviewed the opera
Four Saints in Three Acts, music by Virgil Thomson, libretto by Gertrude
Stein:

> the breakdown in various practical affairs in our immediate times is no
> laughing matter. . . . Accurate parallel is afforded in the apparent break-
> down in . . . the less utilitarian enterprises [like opera]. . . . Gertrude
> Stein's name has been fighting words in the thick of all this. . . . [*Four
> Saints*] will no doubt seem an almost unendurable debacle.[6]

A marked contrast existed between the arts of the twenties and of the
Depression. In the twenties came major changes in esthetic precepts
often involving artistic experimentation and conscious naughtiness as
ends in themselves. The Depression brought forth wholesale questioning of such apparent indulgence, particularly of the art which appeared
intertwined with the reckless, bourgeois spirit of the prior time. Some
among the doctrinaire left sought to maintain some of the experimentalism in their arts as part of their political protest and radicalism which
embraced modern esthetic as well as economic ideals. The political
right sought much the same with of course quite different esthetic and
economic particulars. The majority eschewed extreme solutions, and the
general esthetic tendencies of the thirties involved a moderation of art-
for-art's sake experimentalism. "The time was not for novelty," wrote
composer Virgil Thomson. "It was [a time]," Lewis Mumford recalled,
"when writers and artists were thrown in the streets American life."
While all art strikes a balance between experimentation and communication, in the twenties experimentation often eclipsed communication,
and communication often focused on but a particular avant-garde audience. In the thirties artists generally focused more on communicating
with their audiences than just on the development of their own ideas.
This approach to art typified the era and was the dominant style in the
programs of the New Deal. Throughout the time many artists idealized
their integration with the greater society "in the streets" and showed
much disappointment when this did not yield results culturally or politically.

The work begun under the FERA and the CWA grew to new,
unprecedented levels under the Works Progress Administration. The
WPA and its predecessors contributed to the shift of the arts away from
pure experimentation toward a greater emphasis upon communication.
Unlike previously thriving private institutions which supported or permitted esthetically radical experimentation in the arts they supported, the

government programs generally required communicativeness in language, in visual artistic style, in theatrical and musical performances. The nature of the requirements was quite hazy. The nature of their administration varied between administrators, regions, and artistic genres. As in the National Recovery Administration's aid to industry, the government was not a literal replacement of older arts' institutions. In industry government could influence production levels, wages, and work hours. For many this dangerously broached socialism. For others the vague guidelines did not come within shouting distance of it. Similarly, oversight of the funded arts risked, to some observers, an undue level of government influence upon cultures best left to define themselves. Such unsystematic middle ground was the maddening nature of much New Deal work which frustrated many at the time and since who looked for coherence. Business and government and the arts and government maintained an unsystematic relationship, though it was a relationship of decidedly greater proximity than in any previous era. The political reality, always foremost on Franklin Roosevelt's mind, dictated such a middle ground as the wisest course. And if critics of Roosevelt's intellect are in any way correct, it was the only course possible under his leadership.[7]

One consequence of the haphazardness as well as of the sheer size and complexity of government programs involved conflicts between programs and administrators. Of historic interest, though of minimal political consequence at the time, was a conflict which touched the arts between George Biddle and Edgerton Swartwout. George Biddle, brother of Attorney General Francis Biddle, was a painter and a New Dealer. In 1933 he helped start relief art program for painters under the CWA. When any of his agency's work took place in the District of Columbia, it ran into turf battles with the National Commission of Fine Arts. Generally the CWA was able to carry out its work with but written and largely ineffectual protests from the Fine Arts Commission. The historical irony here was that Biddle was a descendent of Nicholas Biddle, Director of the Bank of the United States under Andrew Jackson. While Nicholas Biddle personified the elite establishment in the 1830's, a century later George Biddle's position was akin to that of the upstart Jacksonians, and his opponent at the imperious Commission—Edgerton Swartwout—was a descendent of Samuel Swartwout, an ardent (as well as notoriously corrupt) Jacksonian.

Other conflicts rose among administrators concerned with the arts within the New Dealer ranks as well. One such fight occurred between WPA Director Harry Hopkins and Edward Bruce. Bruce administered the art projects operating under the auspices of Hans Morgenthau and the Treasury Department, largely involving landscape and mural work on and around Treasury Department buildings. Bruce had first approached Harold Ickes to employ artists in the construction work of the Projects Work Administration, but the always fastidious Ickes rejected the idea as wasteful. Bruce then turned to Treasury Secretary Hans Morgenthau. A devoted landscape gardener, Morgenthau was convinced of the legitimacy of using artists to augment various buildings being constructed under Treasury Department auspices. To this end Bruce apparently lobbied effectively through Mrs. Eleanor Morgenthau, herself an aficionado of painting. Beginning in July, 1935, the Treasury Relief Art Project (TRAP) employed artists to attend to the esthetic aspects of new facilities. Some funding came from Hopkins' WPA. There lay the basis for conflict. In the early days of New Deal artist relief, there had been a problem of artistic standards undercutting the needs of the poor artists. In several instances artists of notoriety, and of relative wealth, received some government money. The esthetic quality of the work was high, but the payment did nothing for poor relief. Ben Shahn was once embarrassed along these lines and sent back the money he received for his work. Later in the WPA, as well as in TRAP, Hopkins was determined to avoid such embarrassments. In TRAP he sought to limit the ratio of employed artists not on relief rolls to 10%. Bruce held 25% to be a wiser figure, more concerned as he was about the inherent artistic quality of the work. Hopkins had his way. Always excitable, Bruce did not take the defeat easily. He separated the Treasury program from the relief rolls altogether and sought several audiences with the President to gain favor. Roosevelt did not respond. Always sensitive to political winds, Morgenthau subsequently phased out Bruce's program. In June of 1936 TRAP employed 356 artists; by October of 1938 only two remained.[8]

In 1935 Congress approved the Works Projects Administration, several months later renamed the Works Progress Administration. Within its administration were the New Deal Arts Projects in writing, theatre, painting, and music, as well as support for several scholarly research ventures. While never quantitatively significant parts of the WPA's overall budget, the Federal arts projects received great attention in the contemporaneous press as well as in subsequent scholarship. It was under the WPA that the many questions involving the arts came forth in full form—relief needs versus artistic considerations, regional favoritism, experimental versus mainstream esthetics, frivolity, waste, burgeoning bureaucracies, inept or arbitrary administration, and the alleged existence of politically subversive activities. For those on the political left who hoped for a metamorphosis in the relations of the arts to society toward a more systematic and ennobling state, the WPA arts programs would prove disappointments, as they were never oriented in any such manner. At the same time, those on the right were also highly critical of many facets of the WPA arts programs. The disappointments and criticisms left and right were important in the political history of the era. They also shed light upon subsequent discussions of the questions involving government support of the arts which continue to the present day.

A constant debate over the administration of the arts projects concerned the degree to which relief considerations should predominate over artistic ones. Should, for example, a needed French horn player be employed in a WPA Music Project orchestra even if he was not in financial straits; or should the orchestra make do with a more needy but manifestly inferior musician or simply do without a horn player? Should a mediocre writer with no money and three children be hired over a proven writer with no dependents and a modicum of savings for a project preparing a travel guide for New Hampshire? Generally the projects set at 10% the extent at which employees could be hired for artistic rather than relief considerations. The essential function of the projects was relief. This fact is pivotal in understanding the significance of the projects and drawing lessons from them in regard to subsequent government initiatives.

With such a relief orientation, much of the work of the arts projects tended toward the esthetically safe and mainstream. Much modern art was more difficult and expensive to prepare, and it risked offending popular (as well as Congressional) sensibilities, with some artistic modernisms linked, often incorrectly, to Left wing politics. On the practical level, in music, for example, with orchestras that could not compare with thriving contemporaries like the NBC Symphony, repertory tended toward the standard symphonic literature from Haydn to Debussy. And the contemporary music that was performed was that of composers like Thomson and Copland who had each gravitated away from the avant-garde fashions of the previous decade toward a more direct, Americana voice. The Music Project was the least risky, politically or esthetically, of the projects. For it was almost exclusively a performance project. It sponsored the writing of no original composition. The Theatre Project sponsored some original musical compositions for its plays, such as Blitzstein's *The Cradle Will Rock*, and that one ran afoul of critics wary of its Leftist leanings. But the Music Project encountered no such problems, for its purview was not creative but, in effect, "re-creative."

Of the arts projects, the Federal Writers' Project appeared to come under some of the heaviest criticism. This came from outside the Project, mainly from Congress, due to anxieties about alleged left-wing activities from within the ranks of Project participants. From the standpoint of the writers themselves, at the time and since, the Project would also prove disappointing. The Project involved a great deal of desultory make work. The main products were the state by state Travel Guides. Virtually none of the Project work was genuinely creative, let alone esthetically innovative. The output of the Writers Project did not constitute a significant force in American letters or take any meaningful place in American literary or intellectual history. Project activities extended none of the lines of poetic and linguistic innovation previously pioneered by such luminaries as T.S. Eliot, Ezra Pound, William Carlos Williams, Wallace Stevens, and e.e. cummings. The Project sponsored no such Depression-era novels as John Steinbeck's *Grapes of Wrath*, no journalistic propaganda work like Ernest Hemingway's *For Whom the Bell Tolls*, nor even such a celebratory novel as Sinclair Lewis' *It Can't Happen Here*.

In regard to subsequent literary developments, the work under the Project does not appear to have served as any sort of backdrop either to the esthetic precepts or to the subject matter of key post-1945 writers like William Styron, Norman Mailer, James Michener, Philip Roth, Saul Bellow, or Gore Vidal. A possible link can be drawn to James Baldwin who built upon the work thought of Ralph Ellison and Richard Wright, in that both were employed by the WPA. But even here the significance of the Project work of Ellison and Wright was minimal with respect to the overall development of each's literary career. Similarly, Kenneth Fearing, Edward Dahlberg, Philip Rahv, May Swenson, Nelson Algren, Anna Botemps, Katherine Dunham, Willard Motley, Frank Yerby and Studs Terkel were all employed by the WPA, but their work on the Project was largely desultory and had little bearing on the significant contributions each subsequently made to American letters. This is not singularly to indict the WPA, for much the same can be said of the irrelevance with respect to their literature of the government work previously performed by Washington Irving, Nathaniel Hawthorne, Herman

Melville, and Robert Lowell. But in the 1930s a key difference was that some WPA leaders regarded their enterprises as ones which could have significant, lasting impacts on American culture, and little of this occurred. Terkel's writings on the Depression and his general commitment to the plight of the common man extended, to some degree perhaps, from his WPA work, but his broader ideological commitments were of deeper significance here. The Travel Guides, an afterthought in the Project drawn up as a sop to critics who feared all the funds would only reach people in the major cities, may have had some later impact upon F.O. Matthiesen's *American Renaissance* and subsequently on Jack Kerouac and, into popular culture, on a late 1950s television program like *Route 66*. But this was a most superficial tapping of what Whitman called "the large unconscious scenery of my land" that some officials envisaged. The broader impact of the Project on American cultural history and creativity was minimal. Commentator Harold Rosenberg held: "There was nothing a writer on the Federal Writers' Project could do that could further his talents or ambitions. . . . [It was] among the lesser players of the Great Depression, every spring threatened with extinction." Responding to any Writers' Project pretensions of literary significance, Florence Kerr lamented: "You must admit, it was one of the higher forms of hypocrisy."[9]

Henry Alsberg was the Director of the Writers' Project from 1935 to 1939. It was under his leadership that visions of widespread, noble results flourished and floundered. His administration was not the most adept, and this further blunted the Project's potential for making a significant contribution to American culture. Malcolm Cowley wrote that Alsberg "was probably not the world's worst administrator, but he might have won an Olympic bronze medal for inspired fumbling. . . . His lines of command were as tangled as a boy's first fishing line." His staff was comprised of friends "whose best years were behind them." Alsberg was an idealist, well read in several languages. He was a capable editor and had considerable powers of inspiration. He had great enthusiasm for his work, possessed and excitedly communicated a vision that the Project could come to portray the nation with a wholeness never before attained. This literary mirroring of the entire nation meant a uniting of neighborhoods, of ethnic groups, of folklore sources, former slaves, and liberal to leftist politics, all then superseding a purely literary context. It would foster a more noble standard of political and social behavior among all who were part of this broadly held sense of culture. Such a vision was very much what artists in many fields hoped the world of esthetics could bring forth from the Depression, and Alsberg was a true believer.[10]

Unfortunately, Alsberg was the sort of person who often talked of books and plays but never got around to writing them. He reveled in his anarchist-bohemian background, and seemed to enjoy the image of the absent-minded father figure. He thus appeared to have no interest in organizational charts or in any systematic delegation of authority. He never even saved carbons of official letters he had written and regularly threw away those his secretary made. One commentator on the Writers' Project—Jere Mangione—himself a Project editor, admitted Alsberg was rather disorganized but clung to a rather sentimental picture of the Director holding affectionately to the potential the Project held for the arts and for the American culture of the Depression era. This generosity in regard to Alsberg was part of an overall predisposition to the very dream Alsberg held so dearly. It was a dream to which the Writers Project never did, and likely never could, devote itself.[11] Alsberg was fired in 1939, and later that year the Emergency Relief Act killed the project on all but state levels.

Generally intellectuals should stay out of power. They tend either to be inept with bureaucratic detail or to compromise their vision. Their involvement with power often blunts the precision of potentially sharp criticisms, robbing society of a more fulsome dialectic of ideas that emerges if intellectuals remain true to their ideals and independent of the machinations of governance. Alsberg's career with the WPA certainly provides evidence here, though the saga of other arts project directors, particularly Hallie Flanagan of the Theatre Project, present contrasting lessons.

In the Writers' Project poor administration was but part of the generally disappointing story. Weak leadership may have aggravated the clashes of ideas and egos, apt to be present among creative people unaccustomed to working in a bureaucracy, clashes which would have occurred to some degree even under the most able leader. Various Project offices, notably New York City's, were rent with divisiveness and factionalism. The New York office had to contend with eleven different unions. Within these bodies and within the Project offices themselves, the various, often precious, stripes of the political left waged war with one another. Strikes, marches, sit-ins, sit-downs, fasts, and fights were regular occurrences. Amidst this, a great deal of collected materials were lost. The Trotskyists and Stalinists were most strident combatants here, and the New York office saw many a shouting match and scuffle. From either side's standpoint any disruption was valid if it would hasten the revolution or forestall the enemy. Some tried to put incriminating leaflets on the desks of colleagues of rivaling perspectives. Malcolm Cowley recalled that on one such occasion the ideologue who had strewn his boss' desk with communist literature called the police. Alas, Cowley noted sardonically, the police arrived late, the leaflets were gone, the worker dismissed, and the revolution postponed.[12] A group of politically non-aligned writers walked out of one steering committee meeting because of a leftist faction's tactics to subvert a decision they did not like even though the majority had approved it. Writer John Cheever had to be sent up to New York from Washington, D.C. to finish the New York Guide because of the mess there.

No place rivaled New York for ideological battles. But problems plagued many of the other Writers' Projects too. The Missouri Project had two utterly incompetent directors. Wyoming, North Dakota, and South Dakota never established a project. In Michigan a young girl applied for a pick-and-shovel job offered to her father, whose health prevented him from taking it. Her application sufficiently moved WPA administrators that she was taken into the Writers' Project. The Director of the Nebraska Project was a paranoid woman named Sheen, who was the mistress of a newspaperman, himself close to Senator Frank Norris. Alsberg let Miss Sheen "run" the Project out of her home, her journalist friend personally conducting some extensive interviews at the Project's headquarters. Elsewhere Alsberg found competent staff who wrote a good Nebraska guide. Vardis Fisher was the Writers' Project for Idaho. "Did the project have literary value?" Fisher asked rhetorically. "Of course, but not much in proportion to the money spent."[13] Fisher wrote the Idaho Guide himself. Given the lack of bureaucracy, it was no accident that his was the first one published. (And he received criticism from some Washington officials for failing to follow the established format.) Fisher also wrote three other books on Idaho for the Project which were sent to Washington, and subsequently lost. Amplifying this matter of ineptness and inefficiency, Raymond Billington, Director of the Massachusetts Project, stated that a well trained team of researchers could have produced the Massachusetts Guide with a quarter of the numbers and a quarter of the time. Vardis Fisher described the Washington office staff as "incompetent and cynical and political." One New York WPA supervisor held: "The Writers' Project was where you dumped the bastard you didn't know what to do with."[14]

In addition to such wastes of time on useful projects, much makework frustrated the employed artists hoping for so much more. Many writers shunned working on the Guide Series and sought other relief jobs in teaching and text book writing. Saul Bellow secured employment at the Chicago office of the Writers' Project and found himself compiling lists of magazines held in the collections of the Newberry Library. He commented that he envied the "interesting" work drawn by colleagues Isaac Rosenfeld and Lionel Abel who, respectively, covered pigeon racing in Chicago and wrote textbooks for high school vocational education curricula. (And the Chicago project was one of the better run offices.) In general the writers resented the tedium, the censorship, the editing of bad prose, the anonymity of group endeavors and unsigned work, laboring with colleagues they often did not like or respect; and all on an enforced 8:00 A.M. to 5:00 P.M. schedule. None of this fit the sensibilities of a typical writer. Many quit the Project as soon as they could afford to.[15]

Despite such problems the Project's historical research was quite valuable. Most famous were the local histories, ethnology, folklore, and narratives of memories of former slaves who had survived into the 1930s. The text books were sorely needed at a time when so many school districts had little money for commercial books. Even here, though, the results were ephemeral, for after the war the stamp of WPA officialdom led the books to be regarded, usually falsely, as either secretly Leftist or excessively pro-FDR, and they quickly fell into disuse. The Guide series had some value, particularly in states in the West where previously the most recent guides told travellers to beware of potential Indian attacks and that bathroom accommodations may be absent. More generally, the series gave some exposure to towns, regions, groups and many other forgotten or neglected aspects of life in America. But even the utility of the guides came largely to naught. The works were completed just as World War II broke out. Few travelled for pleasure during the war, and by the time significant numbers of Americans began such travel again the books were largely outdated, of use to historians and local color novelists but to few others.[16]

The nature of creative writing was and is such that public funding will naturally engender suspicion. The privacy of the craft of writing renders difficult questions of accountability from leaders in the Executive branch as well as in Congress. So straight relief payments to writers to go off on their own and create something was politically out of the question. The Project was plagued by no scandalous wastes of money, but the gap of sensibility between the solitary artist and a government official concerned with accountability was a yawning one only a most skillful and shrewd administrators could bridge. And Alsberg actually enjoyed such confusions and was generally unable to resolve them. In confusion he could deal with individuals, one to one, as he had grown accustomed as an editor and intellectual. His avoidance of confrontation was more a matter of temperament than mere choice. But the consequence was that politicians who had to be dealt with through formal, lawyerly confrontation were ever frustrated. Scouring the books, investigators found the Project's relief rolls to contain the names of several previously convicted of check forgery, claiming indeed that they had previously gained livelihood from writing fiction. Officials grew ever more unsure. Writers were ever wary of funding that may not come and had little faith in their administrators to take care of the matter so they could work productively. Indeed two significant cuts in Congressional appropriations occurred in 1937 and 1939, both of which led to lay offs and greatly hurt morale.

As the Project aroused more and more suspicions and received less and less money, dreams of the funding of genuinely creative writing died. Group projects, research, and travel guides were the order of the day. Relief was always a higher priority than art, so less than excellent writers were on board in large numbers and received the same low wages. With such constrictions and results, even the sentimentally attached Jere Mangione had to conclude: "the experience of the Federal Writers' Project offers no clearly defined lessons for those who champion the cause of governmental subsidy of the arts."[17] The hard public policy questions concerning the utility of government sponsorship of the arts simply receive no answers. Wedded to the Project with which he was intimately involved, Mangione sought at least a neutral rest, since a positive one was not possible. With no such emotional stakes, the poet W.H. Auden drew a different lesson from the Federal Writers' Project. Dubbing it "one of the noblest and most absurd undertakings ever attempted by any state," he noted that contradiction with which state support of the arts compels confrontation. "A state," he pointed out, "can only function bureaucratically and impersonally—it has to assume that every member of a class is equivalent or comparable to every other member—but every artist, good or bad, is a member of a class of one."[18] Once bureaucracy invades the arts esthetic conundrums are inevitable. A key point here is that the writers with whom Auden is concerned were solitary artists. Artists in other genres work differently, however, and possess different sensibilities. The other arts projects of the WPA, studied in conjunction with the Writers' Project, do offer contrasting lessons.

Notes

1. House Report no. 1031, 65th Congress, Third Session.

2. Congressional Record-House of Representatives, 74th Congress, 2d Session, June 18, 1936, pp. 9987-91.

3. Aaron Copland, *The New Music*, 1900-1960, revised and enlarged edition, (New York: W.W. Norton, 1968), p. 160.

4. Oliver Reed and Walter L. Welch, *From Tin Foil to Stereo* (New York: Bobbs Merrill, 1959). pp. 286-87; Dickson Skinner, "Music Goes Into Mass Production," *Harpers*, April, 1939, p. 487; Daniel Gregory Mason, "The Radio vs. the Virtuoso," *American Mercury*, August, 1930, pp. 454-60; and Grace Overmyer, "The Musician Starves," *American Mercury*, June, 1934, pp. 224-31.

5. Among the local arts projects begun by the CWA were: the California Mural Painting Project, the San Francisco Entertainment Project, the Los Angeles Drama Project, the Colorado Springs Music Project, the Connecticut Art Project, the Connecticut Survey of Historic and Scenic Places, the Hartford Concert Orchestra, the Art Project of Illinois, the Cook County Actors Project, the New Orleans Music Project, the Maine Music Project, the Minnesota Music Project, the Nebraska Lancaster County Art Project, the Nevada Art Project, the Concert, New Hampshire Symphony Orchestra, the Portland, Oregon Band, the Pennsylvania Music Project, the Puerto Rico Division of Fine Arts, the South Carolina Richland County Emergency Relief Act Orchestra, and the Vermont Art Project.

6. *Commonweal*, 19 (February 23, 1934), p. 525.

7. see, for example, Paul Conkin, *The New Deal* (Arlington Heights, Ill.: AHM Publishing Corporation, 1975), *passim.*

8. see Kathleen O'Connor McKenzie, *The New Deal for the Artists,* (Princeton University Press, 1973), p. 42.

9. see Harold Rosenberg, "Anyone Who Could Write English," *New Yorker*, vol. 48, January 20, 1973, pp. 99-102; Malcolm Cowley, "The Federal Writers' Project," *New Republic*, Vol. 167, October 21, 1972, pp. 23-6.

10. Ibid.

11. Jere Mangione, *The Dream and the Deal, The Federal Writers' Project*, 1935-1943 (Boston: Little Brown, 1972.)

12. Malcolm Cowley, *New Republic*, October 21, 1972, p. 24; see also Mangione, pp. 170-2.

13. Mangione, pp. 201-8.

14. Mangione, pp. 85-6 and 202-08.

15. Harold Rosenberg, "Anyone Who Could Write English," *New Yorker*, Vol. 48, January 20, 1973, pp. 99-102; see also Mangione, p. 123.

16. Penkhower, p. 247.

17. Mangione, p. 373.

18. quoted in Rosenberg, "Anyone Who Could Write English," p. 100.

The Theatre, Art, and Music Projects: Contrasting Lessons

Many debilitating existential questions plagued the Writers' Project. These questions involved definitions of what precisely was (is) a writer, painter, musician, or actor. The overriding priority of providing relief mitigated the debilitation to some degree here, as the purely artistic vagaries within the question could and did take lower priority to that of providing help to the needy. But the priority of relief itself brought on other problems, the hiring of convicted check forgers being but one of the more noteworthy. In addition to such slips, the simple varying of standards between state projects yielded further troubles. Within the variations lay not just the differences between administrators over procedures but also over the conflict over relief versus art.

While such potential frustrations lay in waiting for the administrators in all the arts projects, they appear to have affected the Writers' Project most. The Federal Theatre Project showed a very different picture. While the Federal Writers' Project built little upon previous innovations in the historical development of American literature and seemed to feed into very few post-1945 directions, the Federal Theatre Project was a very significant part of the development of the theatre in America. Hallie Flanagan, Director of the Theatre Project, was a significant factor here. Flanagan knew the theatre thoroughly, as well as Henry Alsberg knew writing and editing, but she also stayed atop all the details of her office. An established playwright and the first woman ever to be awarded a Guggenheim Fellowship, Flanagan held the respect of everyone connected with the theatre, a respect she maintained as Director while she dealt capably with all the people and issues on the artistic side of the

Project ledger. She also worked tirelessly with Congress as well as with local officials to minimize suspicions about waste and about alleged left-wing political activities. She was not completely successful here, but sufficiently so to maintain morale within the project and to keep Congress from making any significant budget cuts until 1939. In hindsight, feminists and old-fashioned sexists could each attempt to account for Flanagan's success on the basis of her gender. Congressional watchdogs may have thought less seriously about her than they did about Alsberg. Traditional gentlemanly norms of behavior may have stifled potential criticisms when she testified before them. But gender was likely not a great issue, and Flanagan never raised the matter, then or in retrospect. As with respect to many successful women of eras before the mid 1960s, feminist modes of analysis appear to cloud with presentism as much as they elucidate various people and times in question. Flanagan's success stemmed simply from the respect she held within her field and from her effective work habits. She travelled tirelessly and organized many local theatre projects which, with her guidance, were staging plays within months of the creation of the Federal Project. She rooted out substandard work and eradicated much of it. She overcame professional objections to charity as well as Broadway's and other major enclave's objections to competition. Under her leadership the Project employed over 13,000 people, by far the largest of the arts projects.

Like Alsberg, Flanagan held to certain ideals and had visions about what her Project could accomplish. Compared to Alsberg, however, her dreams were more realistic, though by no means myopic. Flanagan's vision focused on the theatre itself. When she began her work she knew that theatre had not genuinely penetrated many regions of the United States, and she saw the very real possibility that the Project could lead to a more national purview for the theatre. To some extent she succeeded, for many small towns and remote areas had no standing theatres before the 1930s and have had them since. One writer called this program "the first attempt to bring theater to the masses since Thespis was banished from Athens and took to the provinces."[1] While obvious hyperbole, such statements revealed the degree of enthusiasm many held for the WPA initiatives as well as how well Flanagan's work sat with such commentators.

While Alsberg hoped the work of the Writers' Project could somehow effect a complete metamorphosis in the sensibilities of the entire nation, Flanagan never considered such a far-flung impact. Like any artist she believed her art would affect audiences, but the nature of the impact and any resulting political or social thought or action was a matter for the individuals in the audience to decide for themselves. Such matters could not be prescribed or predicted. Theatre could thus become in her mind more of a national cultural force, but what the nature of that force would be was less the issue for her. More down-to-earth in vision, the nature of theatre work under Flanagan also contrasted with the less successful Writers' Project.

The spectre of a subversive writer working on his or her own, with minimal oversight, while enjoying Federal support, aroused suspicions from Congressmen as well as from the public at large. Consequently the Writers' Project compelled work done in offices in collaborative frameworks which, while not completely at odds with the general pattern of writers' habits, did not mesh with the routine and sensibilities of many hired for the Project. The collaborative and "inspectable" dimensions did not need to be so contrived in the Theatre Project. For generally the staging of a play is, by nature, collaborative and takes place in an arena which can be readily opened to any who seek to view the proceedings. This arouses fewer suspicions and requires fewer preemptive contrivances. The work done could then involve actual theatre work, with no demoralizing measures clearly contrived but to stave off official, often artless oversight.

In artistic content too, the collaborations in the Theatre Project veered away from the avant-garde experiments of the 1920s. The emphasis, which needed little official enforcement, seemed naturally to emphasize communicativeness over obscure expressionism. It was a fortunate coincidence of commonality between artistic convictions of the theatre people and the dictates for reification that come with government subvention and which at the time were strong among the general public.

Like the Music Project, the Theatre Project could also present their work to the public in manners which made people and their Congressional representatives gain a sense of return on their investment. The Writers' tomes sitting on library or store shelves did not have the same impact as a public performance. The Theatre and Music Project could also charge admission for performances. Ticket prices were generally low (normally thirty cents, and many performances were free). This aroused angry charges of unfair competition from private theatre and musical organizations. Otherwise, the device, again not a contrivance, lent an image that the Congressional expenditures were seed money rather than the straight relief which seemed more the case with the writers. While many of the Writers' Project's works subsequently sold to libraries as well as to the public at large, the return of money appeared more vicarious, one which tended to serve an elite. The direct purchase of a ticket for a government sponsored show appeared a more acceptable expenditure.

While the concerns for the potentially negative imagery surrounding a solitary writer led the Writers' Project to contrive often desultory procedures which restricted the normal habits and parameters of a professional writer, the Federal funding of theatre fostered experimentation which continued many key esthetic developments in American theatre. Several innovations occurred which likely would have taken much longer, if ever, through traditional organizational means. On a technical level, electronic lighting boards with dimmer controls and backstage projection were two innovations that came with the Project.[2] Generally the Project could not easily foster such technical innovations, for by law ninety percent of the Project's budget had to be spent on salaries, so lighting, costumes, and other technical crafts had to be held at a minimal level. Other innovations occurred in genre and form, however. A Children's Theatre commenced under the Project, and performed before 250,000 people. A Marionette Theatre also began under the project, and its performances drew 1.5 million over two years. These were not new ideas, but they received far more funding and rapidly touched many more geographic areas than ever before. In 1937 an experimental version of *MacBeth* was staged with an all African-American cast. 144 performances were staged; 130,000 people attended, grossing the Project $40,000. African-American theatre and actors never reached such wide audiences before this Project support, and it would be many years before they would reach such levels again.[3]

With the availability of funds and a generally hospitable environment, the Project saw many stimulating collaborations among imaginative writers, directors, actors, and technical staff. One Project play in 1936, for example, *The Horse Eats Hat*, involved writer Edwin Denby's adaptation of a comedy by the French playwright Eugene Labiche; production was by John Houseman, direction and lead acting by Orson Wells, music by Virgil Thomson, and lighting by Abe Fedder. Unlike the writers, where collaboration was out of the ordinary and often yielded resistance, ego clashes and demoralization, such exchange was more the norm in the theatre. The Project heightened a vital process already inherent in the art form. Some of the new work, most famously *One Third of a Nation* and a staging of Sinclair Lewis' *It Can't Happen Here*, also served to underscore and celebrate the centrist tendencies in the American political arena.

Some new works in the Project were more challenging in regard to political norms. Here the Project ran afoul of critics. Even here, however, ironic conundrums as well as straight resistance resulted. Marc Blitzstein's opera/singspeil *The Cradle Will Rock*, for example, was a Theatre Project play which depicted the struggles of labor unions and organizers. Such content raised hackles of conservative Congressmen. Sensitive to such concerns Project administrators had shifted the focus of the Project's work from "relevant" theatre in 1936 and 1937 to "regional" theatre in 1937 and 1938. Blitzstein's politically "relevant" work was caught in this shift. The Project's New York leadership felt sufficient pressure to close the theatre before *The Cradle*'s 1937 premier. The story of its closing further illustrates the nuances and complexities in the operation of the arts and consequently in the relationship of the arts and government. *The Cradle* was to open at the Maxine Elliott Theatre in New York. Theatre Project officials made their decision and bolted the theatre doors only hours before the opening performance, blocking access to all stage effects and musical instruments. The performers, musicians, the opening night audience, and Mr. Blitzstein all arrived and could not enter. Blitzstein then led the actors, musicians and audience down to the nearby Venice Theatre. With a blank stage, no props, and no instruments but the theatre's upright piano, Blitzstein had to improvise. He reduced the stage movements to a minimum, presenting the scenario more starkly. Sitting at the piano, creating a reduction of his orchestral score from memory, Blitzstein decided to augment the forcibly thin accompaniment with verbal explanations to the audience. In subsequent reviews, critics raved at such an innovation in the presentation of musical theatre. It was indeed an unusual approach, but as much a product of panic as of esthetic conviction. Perhaps the dialectic between the ideologies of WPA critics and artists like Blitzstein brought forth a new esthetic, anticipated by neither one.

The same sorts of political tensions existed in the Federal Art Project. Much of the work of the Art Project that caught the public eye involved the painting of murals on major public buildings. Painting in America had departed, though not completely, from the abstract experimentation of the 1920s toward a more visually realistic style which often celebrated the life of mainstream America. Yet some of the mural work contained visual snippets which extolled the virtues of radical political ideologies. A funded mural by Emile Zakheim, for example, displayed a chaotic urban street scene with the unemployed and dispossessed look-ing desperate and bewildered. But in one section of the mural the peo-ple's countenances and manners appeared more calm and directed, and they had in their hands copies of *The Daily Worker*.

As in much of the nation's painting in the 1930s, realistic, Americana art dominated the Art Project, though there were some government spon-sored abstract works. Through the 1920's the country's mainstream crit-ics and audiences had resisted the tendency of modern art toward abstractionism. While many exceptions certainly existed, a strong cor-relation lay between abstract painting and radical politics while realistic painting was identified with the political middle of the road. In the 1930s this continued, and Americana paintings were generally seen as patriotic while much abstract work was linked to New York City, to Europe, and to socialism. Many of the abstract radicals saw themselves as part of this movement and used their art to effect an esthetic counter-point to a social and political movement which would bring about a more just society upon the ashes of the depression. They saw the real-ists both accepting the established esthetic order and either apologizing for the political status quo or failing to grasp the radical solutions which the desperate times required. Particularly in the early 1930s this radical view dominated among artists in New York. As in the Writers' Project, this would later cast a pall over the Art Project when Congressional con-servatives began to hunt reds. Some official criticism of the Americanists arose concerning their seemingly uncritical patriotism being proto-fascist, but that was minor compared to the red hunting. By the late 1930s the radicals were also rent with factionalism. They were not terribly popular outside their own ranks and appeared a somewhat self pitying lot.[4]

The esthetic adventurousness of the Art Project participants varied between the Project's divisions. The artists of Easel Division under Joseph Solman were the more esthetically avant-garde compared, for example, to the artists under Edward Lansing of the Murals Division. Illustrating the link between politics and esthetics here, Solman was sharply critical of the muralists' hackneyed, pedestrian works, be they Americana scenes or proletarian celebrations. (And it was the artists of the Easel Division who fell under the suspicion of the Dies Commission, particularly in 1940 when some of them balked at condemning the Russian invasion of Finland.)

Quantitatively, the left leaning work in the Project was not terribly significant, but it gained much notoriety and criticism from both the

Congress and the press. Meanwhile the Americana art ran afoul of certain influential critics. The holdovers of the chic, largely New York based critical community were fatiguingly negative in their treatment of the mainstream. They pooh-poohed the celebratory realistic and nationalistic art of the 1930's as a throwback to bygone times in regard both to style as well as to philosophy. But their views were largely *sui generis*, though they would continue to plague the career of such a notable as Thomas Hart Benton well beyond the decade of the thirties. Benton, as well as Grant Wood and Thomas Craven, were perhaps the most famous artists whose sensibilities fit the precepts of the Art Project. For some painters like Jackson Pollock and Mark Rothko, who would become among the most famous American abstract expressionists in the 1940s, the realistic paintings they created in the 30's under WPA auspices and funding would become sources of embarrassment.[5] The Art Project leadership indeed sided with the realistic precepts of Benton and his colleagues, openly discouraging abstraction. By the late 1930's, with the disarray of the Left and the attacks of the right, this choice appeared wise from both political and artistic standpoints. That the art world after 1945 took a turn toward abstractionism rendered the work of the 30's precious and a detour with respect to the main course of 20th-century American painting. Such turns can never be foreseen. Further, it raises many questions as to what ought be the place of the government, assuming it ought play a role in the arts, with respect to avant garde movements. Should government lend support to work of a shocking nature, at times even intentionally so, to mainstream sensibilities? Conversely, will genuinely radical sensibilities be compromised with government involvement? These were major questions in the 1930s, and they would reappear in subsequent decades.

For better and worse, Art Project Director Holger Cahill led the movement toward the mainstream. He sought, in his words, to lift art "from its limited circle of admirers" and to divest it "of its esoteric and precious nature." "Modernism," he declared, "is related to the worship of esthetic fragments torn from their social contexts, and to the idea of art for the select few." Painter Thomas Craven echoed these sentiments when he contended: "Only that art which draws its inspiration from the body of the people can be good art and mean something to the people for whom it has been created."[6]

While the wisdom in the Art Project's preference for realism and its generally celebratory Americanism was and is a matter for debate, an undeniably positive offshoot of the work involved a growing concern for the indigenous art of previously little known sectors of the American art world. In addition to the exposure of art from neglected geographic areas, particular craft heritages also gained broad new levels of exposure. Here the Art Project paralleled the Writers' Project's unearthing of neglected traditions. But, more like the Theatre Project, it was successful in enlivening the appreciation of art in these regions. On a technical level, as well, the Art Project was responsible for the fostering or acceleration of several innovations. Acrylic paint, for example, was developed under the Art Project's auspices. Silkscreening for posters and signs gained great impetus as a result of the WPA, as did carborundum etching. The Art Project also pioneered much work in lithography and color lithography and their many uses in various media. This increased popular interest in and consumption of prints. It also bridged a gap between the old etching societies of pre-Depression eras and the graphic arts of the 1950s and 1960s.[7]

Like the Writers' Project participants, the painters, sculptors, and other artists who worked in the Art Project sometimes found themselves working with inadequate supplies, having to contend with arbitrary and often artless criteria in the selection of colleagues, and facing petty bureaucratic standards and controls over their work which interfered with what they saw as their Constitutional rights of free expression. Like the writers, they complained mightily about all these matters. In all the projects, the fact of public funding invited criticisms from outsiders, some informed, some not, which broached questions involving the legitimacy of censorship where Federal support was present. This would arise repeatedly in the thirties, as well as in subsequent eras.

Notes

1. "The WPA Creates New Theatergoers," *Literary Digest*, August 29, 1936, p. 781.

2. John O'Connor and Lorraine Brown, *Free, Adult, and Uncensored* (Washington, DC: 1978), pp. 5-7.

3. see Jane DeHart Mathews, *The Federal Theatre, 1935-1939, Plays, Relief, and Politics* (Princeton: Princeton University Press, 1967). pp. 75-6.

4. see Francis O'Connor, *The New Deal Art Projects: An Anthology of Memoirs* (Washington: The Smithsonian Institution Press, 1972), p. 320; Matthew Baigell, *The American Scene Painting of the 1930s* (New York, 1974), p. 55.

5. O'Connor, p. 117.

6. Martha Davidson, "The Government as Patron of the Art," *Art News* (October 10, 1936), p. 141; Baigell, pp. 54 and 59.

7. see Francis O'Connor, *Federal Support for the Visual Arts* (New York: New York Graphics Society, 1986), p. 54.

The Heritage of the New Deal Art Programs

The specific political and esthetic nature of the criticisms of publicly funded art would vary from era to era. During the 1930s several basic criticisms often came forth. Because some bureaucrats could be rather loose in their definitions and grant funds to people who did not truthfully qualify for assistance, check forgers passing as fiction writers, for example, many criticized the lack of standards in the WPA projects. In counterpoint to such laxity, excessive rigor of definition also ran risks. Here administrators could easily include the best in various fields who were often the least in need, compromising the priority of relief. Administrators would invite further criticism here by overlooking the marginally capable who had had to work in other endeavors to make financial ends meet and then presented employment records which disqualified them from assistance. Rules and standards also varied between locales. Bureaucrats, administrators, Congressmen, artists and the public could all be frustrated.

Generally the WPA avoided supporting artistic frauds. Existential and deconstructionist *cul de sac's* over what constitutes art or an artist, did not muddy critical senses to the degree they have in more recent times in either public or private institutions. The chief problem involved the continuing tendency to help established talent more than the "starving" artist. This was a problem for which no single solution arose. And it was not by any means a matter unique to the arts in the panorama of New Deal activities. Far more notable in the public mind in this vein, for example, was the work of the Agricultural Adjustment Administration in which the middling and wealthy farmers gained far morc than the sharecroppers.

Other problems in the arts projects concerned the risks of damages to institutions barely surviving in the private sector. It was indeed difficult for a private orchestra or theatre to compete with one sponsored by the Music or Theatre Project charging but thirty cents a ticket. Charges over frivolity and waste continued to arise as well, even though the combined WPA projects spent but twenty-six million dollars over their seven and eight years of existence. From within the projects, critics in Congress, as well as from the general public continuously raised the question of the utility of such expenditures. The degree of criticism from the project workers themselves, particularly in the Writers' Project, was unique to the depression era. The duality of goals in the programs directed toward both artistic and relief ends made virtually inevitable such criticisms, especially in instances where artistic concerns clearly took second priority.

The question of utility raised from the general public and their representatives was nothing new. Such swipes came from as far back as the 1820s from Rep. John Randolph and from politicians in every generation thereafter. Such criticism is difficult to debate systematically. The pro and con positions each commence with irreconcilable premises. The critics ultimately question the utility of the arts or then whether the government has any business being involved with them at all. The other side simply assumes the validity of the arts. Proof of either view here is difficult if not impossible. The utility or disutility of the arts can only be asserted, and any assertion, if sincere, rests largely on sensibilities ultimately psychological in nature, born perhaps from experience. (Any insincere view is usually based on a cynical political considerations, and thus need not be considered in artistic or philosophical terms at all.) Supporters accept the utility of the arts as a given and balk at any questioning of utility as preposterous. For those in positions of political power, the responses to questions of utility tend to lead merely to political calculations—independent of whether the criticism is philosophically valid, do the criticisms reflect a sufficiently sizable body of voters to necessitate significant adjustments? In the thirties, New Deal leaders reckoned the public was supportive, or at least sufficiently ambivalent. So criticisms of waste could be largely ignored or handled rhetorically.

The chief point of criticism which prompted a significant political response involved allegations of left wing activism and propaganda in the funded works of art and literature as well as among artists themselves. A rhetorically independent, though ultimately related point of criticism which would also prove significant here concerned the projects excessive focus of expenditures and attention on but a few large cities. Such charges made for good copy in the press and provided anti-Roosevelt forces with some rhetorical ammunition. Emil Zakheim and Marc Blitzstein were but two examples here. The New York Writers' Project had many avowed leftists. The sympathetic Jere Mangione admitted, for example, that New Yorker Kenneth Fearing was "closely identified with the Stalinist faction."[1] In retrospect the danger posed by such people to lead a revolution that would overthrow both the government and the capitalist economy hardly appears significant. But whether or not the dangers were significant, fears abounded, and conservative politicians knew a great deal of political capital could be drawn out of such a situation. In 1938 Congressman Martin Dies of Texas thus formed a committee aimed at discrediting Roosevelt and the New Deal. In 1937 Roosevelt had committed perhaps his greatest political blunder with the Court packing controversy. Republican opponents sensed he was at last vulnerable, and Dies went to work, using the WPA as a pet target. Why the pendulum swung as it did in regard to the intensity of fears of "reds" is a vexing one. The evidence was always there to be rhetorically exploited. There were always rightist extremists preaching the anti-communist gospel. The chief question is why such preachers gained followers when they did (1919, 1938, 1947-53). It is too simple to retort that they simply exploit ignorant voters, for this does not explain why such pleas work in some eras and not in others. Anxieties over an economic downturn or over the possibility of one seem to have lain among people whenever these scares grew. In the thirties the political right had been dormant since 1932 and made a comeback between 1938 and 1940. The apparent indulgences of the left in the New Deal appeared a liability. Congressman J. Parnell Thomas of New Jersey called the Writers' Project "a hotbed of communists."[2] Records were combed and the various examples of waste and fraud were held up out of context for ridicule. The work of the Dies Committee, along with the shrill criticisms of other conservative critics like Frederick Busby of Illinois and George Dondero of Michigan, presaged the McCarthy era, and its work provided a pivotal backdrop to the Relief Bill of 1939-1940 which abolished the Theatre Project, reduced the other Projects to a minimum, and transferred them to the states. They limped into the war years and died in 1943. During the war, when the government sought to employ various artists to create canvases and other artifacts which, for example, could help maintain the patriotism and morale of the troops, these same Congressmen spoke in opposition, fearing hidden Leftist hues would creep into the work.

While the tone and motivation of Dies Committee and other conservatives had cynical and destructive elements, the broader and vexing context is that such complications are invariably a consequence of government support of artistic endeavors. The outright censorship of the arts has always been minimal in the United States, and indeed some, by no means all, of the political conservatives who were bent upon rooting out communists from the government Projects would be among the most vehement critics of those who would censor on the basis of the First Amendment. (Indeed such a case could be a good test of their Constitutional sincerity.) But because the New Deal marked the first time of any extended government initiative on behalf of the arts, it also marked the first time the arts became significant parts of the political panorama. Quantitatively the levels of leftist involvement in WPA projects was minimal. Beyond the question of actual affiliations, the political culture of the nation was not conducive to the ideas of the Left. For every person who read Steinbeck's *Grapes of Wrath* and felt any class-based anger or urge to act, many were equally moved by Sinclair Lewis' *It Can't Happen Here.* To judge whether people ought to have chosen one path or the other here is a matter for each citizen/historian.

In contrast to the fears of the Dies Committee and other conservatives, the possibility of the Left actually bringing about a revolution and successfully overthrowing the capitalist economy was quite remote. But the hopes on the Left, as well as the fears on the right, were strong amidst the desperate conditions of the thirties. And for those on the right who resented their newly marginalized status in national politics, fears of Marxists constituted a public sensibility to be exploited. Any hints of "subversion" in government-sponsored work like the WPA became easy and irresistible targets. The number of people who suffered as a result of these attacks was not large. This is not to excuse or even minimize the injustices suffered. But without the WPA the quantity of suffering among those in the arts would likely have been yet greater. The sad but overriding point here is that such political sniping, in one form or another, is bound to happen whenever the government becomes involved in the arts. And the calculation of economic deprivation versus political suffering due to government inaction or action is a cruel but inevitable calculation for those considering the issue.

Government sponsored art is, by definition, politicized. Such a situation engenders a tightrope which arts administrators must traverse. It is not a question of whether but how well they walk it. The successful here usually show themselves to have done some preemptive work with regard to politically sensitive activities with a conveyed sense of where boundaries are systematically to be set. Surrounding this must lie a context which demonstrates a sense and understanding of artistic quality and sincerity. The credentials of the administrator must be artistically and politically impeccable to underscore this successfully.

In the WPA the successes of Holger Cahill in the Art Project and, even more, Hallie Flanagan in the Theatre Project reveal this. Henry Alsberg's lesser success in the Writers' Project reveals this counterfactually. Flanagan and Cahill were both thoroughly in command of all the details within their respective projects. They had gained the highest respect of the professionals in their fields, so they could pass reasoned judgment upon the worthiness of many initiatives, eliminating problems with esthetic discernment, before outside Congressional oversight entered the fray and handle matters with less esthetic sense. The nature of the different arts provides additional insights into the successes and failures of the New Deal Arts experiences, hence into the lessons they provide. The solitary artist seemed somehow potentially more dangerous than did artists working in groups. There are few means by which to check the solitary writing of fiction or scholarship while it is in progress. It is but paper or, even more ethereally, ideas. But a mural in progress or a play in rehearsal can be readily examined. Artistic genres like theatre where collective activities are natural components of the creative processes could more readily thrive under government sponsorship. They more naturally fit bureaucratic dictates and answered public questions.

The theatres and concert halls also charged nominal admission fees under the WPA. The art exhibits could have but did not. Such features were, again, not structural contrivances. And they lent a sense of money well invested to sufficient numbers of budget minded citizens and officials to hold recalcitrant critics isolated and at bay. The returns from writing projects come forth in less participatory fashions. They can be read publicly but even that could appear a contrivance. And any public ceremony honoring the authors does not "consume" the work the public sponsored. Books' normal mode of consumption yields less of a sense of public involvement and applause than does a successful play or concert. Their economic return via sales can be quantitatively significant and often greater than the returns from the low-priced tickets to the WPA plays and concerts, but the public sense of economic return from books has a different effect. Books, writers, publishers and the whole literary world appear more a commerce among elites. This was especially so in the 1930s. Thus the charging of fees for the procurement of government publications seemed to perpetuate the activities of this elite world more than serve the general population. The books' availability in public libraries provided little mediation here. In an age of Depression when relief was a priority, the direct psychic relief to someone who attended a funded musical or theatre performance sat much better with the public than did the knowledge of a book they could go to a library and read. Amplifying this issue in the context of more recent times, beginning in the 1980s, with the popularization of the VCR, enterprises renting and selling videotapes have thrived. A library could never thrive if it rented books. Indeed public libraries have closed in significant numbers in the late 1980s and 1990s, despite charges being virtually nil, in large part because of the growth of video stores. Books are, or appear, the leisure of elites. The mass public prefers other art forms, and the market responds. Thus there is a paradox of a popularly accessible, free genre of art—literature—being regarded as elite, while one whose public access is to some degree regulated by wealth thrives among the mass public. This same sensibility of books as elite articles held as well in the thirties and exacerbated the problems of publicly supported writing in contrast to funded theatre, musical concerts, or art.

A great aid to the successful acceptance of the public support of artistic endeavors in the 1930s lay further in the confluence of the tendency of government dictates and the general esthetic precepts of the age. Much of the painting, music, literature of the 1930s was marked by a decided return to realism. The naughty experimentalism of the 1920s had grown passe. Abstractionism, atonalism, seriality and other such modernist modes ill fit an era beset by enormous economic difficulties. Independent of such swings in artistic sensibilities, the Federal government would have had a difficult time justifying the support of art that appeared impenetrable to the average audience. It had to gravitate toward art which emphasized communicativeness. And the key was that this natural demand of government harmonized well with many, by no means all, the artistic sensibilities of the era. This was a fortunate situation in the 1930s when the government could easily mirror the arts, a state of affairs which cannot be forced. The absence of such harmony would cause problems in later eras when the government shied away from supporting avant garde art, which was more at the center of the art world's predilections, and favored a more generally popular and allegedly more artless mainstream.

Another service of which the WPA programs could boast involved bringing the arts to areas theretofore virtually untouched by such cultural genres. This heritage echoes little into subsequent ages given the penetration of many private institutions since 1945 and given even more the impact of television.

The general heritage of the WPA arts programs yields no single lessons for subsequent efforts with respect to Federal activism in the arts. The setting of extreme economic depression limits the applicability of that era's theories for activism. The newness of availability of much traditional culture lent a freshness to many activities that a government in a television culture could never approach. The glaring needs for such basic commodities as guide books filled easily definable social voids that simply do not exist in more advanced, saturated times. Thus much of the work of the Writers and Music Projects would have been difficult to justify in any time since. Where the government programs were successful in Theatre and Art lay in the simultaneous nurturing of elements of the avant garde and capturing regional and national themes. This required a certain level of esthetic linkage between the two which cannot be compelled. It also required bureaucratically able as well as esthetically inspirational leadership from such figures as Cahill and Flanagan. They needed to manage the many egos of artists and satisfy the no less ego driven complications brought forth by Congressmen.

Whether the esthetic precepts of the avant garde and the public at large can be brought into any uneasy harmony is always an issue for any government officials concerned with the arts, as it is for people in arts organizations in the private sector. Here the New Deal provides only the well-known lesson that this is a very difficult task. If the public do not openly suspect the artists and scholars, suspicions always seem to lurk, suspicions which skillful politicians will invariably exploit. It happened in the 30s; it happened before; and it would resurface later. While politicians will regularly break any calm here, so will many of the artists themselves. With politicians it may be sad, from a Jeffersonian standpoint, that some will cater to low common denominators of popular thought for the sake of extending power. With artists the lamentability has as many psychological as philosophical moorings. Artists have always tended to be non-conformists, each a class of one, as W.H. Auden reflected. Someone will always challenge the norms, and when the norm involves a large government, challenges will always engender great political waves. Those empowered to administer the arts then must be prepared to be attacked from either side. It happened in the 30s, and it has happened since.

Notes

1. Mangione, p. 177.
2. Mangione, p. 290.

Into the Cold War and onto the Political Stage: The Federal Government and the Arts since 1945

In his preface to *Portrait of a Lady* Henry James speculated upon the interrelationship of the artist and society. Noting the nature of the community of artists, what he called "the house of fiction," James contended the house has "not one window, but a million." From each window comes one artist's vision of the world, each true unto itself (assuming the artist's integrity) but each different, sometimes slightly sometimes markedly. The "human scene," James then declared, is "the choice of subject" in the work of art; "the perceived aperture . . . is the literary form." The scene and aperture "are, singly or together, as nothing without the posted presence of the watcher—without, in other words, the consciousness of the artist." The infinite variety of scenes denotes the artists' freedom. Each's consciousness provides his or her moral reference. In James' day the moral references themselves varied nearly as much as the scenes. If any commonality of reference existed it could constitute a zeitgeist which could be ennobling (or degrading).[1]

To James any such commonalities were, above all, matters which should never be subject to any sort of social or political compulsion. Sensitivity to the rigidity of his own culture in late nineteenth-century America, James achieved notoriety as he sought freedom from any unduly taut geographic or national mooring. The notion of any sort of compulsion is indeed abhorrent to most any artist. In the United States this proclivity among artists has regularly harmonized with broader political traditions against such force, traditions well rooted in American political culture. In glorious seventeenth-century earthiness, Roger

Williams had declared that "compulsion stinks in the nostrils of God." The whole Jeffersonian tradition of minimal government further rests upon the same notion. And that most powerful political strain combined with the proclivities of James and artists like him to contribute toward a disdain for any official orthodoxy about the arts. A mere few of James million windows could not and should not receive any artificial notoriety, even through well-intentioned public support. Likely, James would have agreed here, though, just as likely, he would have added disenthralled points with respect to the judgments of the artistic marketplace. To James artistic excellence was, *à la* Schopenauer, a thing in itself. The artist could only seek it alone. Judgments were for posterity, and there was nothing sacrosanct there either.

In the early twentieth century, with the desire for the United States to assume a position of greater respectability in the world of culture, pressures grew for some official activism in the arts. Little occurred, however, aside from specific activities in Washington, D.C. Arguing against official activism, in addition to continuing resistance along Jeffersonian lines, was the fear that certain European-focused elite genres and traditions (i.e., certain "windows") would receive undue favoritism. This state of affairs remained until the Depression. Then some of the obstacles fell away. The motives for support shifted from the achievement of international prestige toward national relief, affirmation and survival. Anti-Jeffersonian support for government activism held the majority voice in government. The commonality of economic problems lowered many previously powerful cultural barriers of class and region. On the political left many still saw such class-based barriers but held that a common ideology, with cultural as well as economic components, could and should be forged.

Whether of the doctrinaire left or of the more Americana middle, a significant group of cultural activists and politicians felt a national culture, albeit conceived in different forms, could be supported and nurtured with the gains, over and above economic benefits, far outweighing the dangers. Not all were pleased with such results as those of the WPA programs. But even such critics would acknowledge that the dominant political sensibilities of the era permitted far greater activism than ever before. One historian, deeply critical of the unsystematic nature of the New Deal, in effect summarized the role of New Deal critics when he declared that such people belong in the pulpit or the classroom but are too clear headed to master the soothing art of the fireside chat.[2]

Considering the WPA programs—their remarkable internal haziness or their failure to forge any sort of national culture or even to provide groundwork for any later such forgings, such retrospective disdain for Roosevelt and the New Deal's internal incoherence is certainly substantiated. At the time, however, some idealists, politically left and middle, held some certainty over the real or potential existence of an identifiable national culture. Outside the world of 1930's politics many began discussing such notions. Before the Depression discussions of "culture" tended to focus on artistic elites, largely American counterpoints to European high culture. Others had asserted an American uniqueness in mass culture, but often in a sneering manner. Ezra Pound, for example, wrote: "If America has given or is to give anything to general aesthetics it is presumably an aesthetic of machinery or porcelain baths, of cubic rooms painted with Ripolin, hospital wards with patent dust-proof corners and ventilating appliances."[3] In the 1930s many intellectuals pressed for a new mass culture that was truly national and not apart from certain elites. Diverse artists like Aaron Copland, Thomas Hart Benton, Grant Wood, Carl Sandberg, John Steinbeck, and Thornton Wilder sought this in their respective fields. In more general thoughts about culture, intellectuals like Ruth Benedict, Margaret Mead, Franz Boaz and John Dewey began defining culture in conscious contrast to the belleletre notions of prior times. "As long as art is the beauty parlor of civilization," wrote Dewey, "neither art nor civilization is secure."[4] "Culture" came to be regarded more as an anthropological phenomenon, as Mead put it: "the learned ways of behavior characteristic of a group." This did not exclude traditional high culture, though some have since abused the perspective and indulged in reverse snobbery, but it brought forth a new context that neglected class distinctions and thus championed democracy.

Utilizing this vision of a national culture insuring democratic political ideals and avoiding pitfalls of counter elitism and superficial smugness, Robert Hutchins of the University of Chicago was among the leading educators who sought to reify culture in educational curricula. In his mind, there was a common culture for all, and the pursuit of such complicated commonality served a noble social purpose of promoting a democratic culture, particularly as that culture was growing diffuse and found itself tugged by anti-democratic impulses at the political fringes. Then and since many have argued with Hutchins' assertion of a common heritage capable of embodiment in a university curriculum. Hutchins saw such rigor as humanistic and liberating. Schooling would enable each generation to build upon the past and not merely flail and repeat past errors out of ignorance or narcissism. Hutchins was not able to achieve all he wished though he did have some success at Chicago, and his example significantly influenced other institutions. Hutchins' conception of a commonality of culture came in an era when geography and class barriers appeared to be breaking down. His efforts reflected and sought to extend the perceived consensus about a mass and democratic culture.

In retrospect some of Hutchins' efforts appear right wing. Indeed they engendered many of the same questions conservative Allan Bloom's *Closing of the American Mind* would broach fifty years later. Hutchins wrote of a "common human nature" conveyed through studies which connect us with the best that man has thought. "Real unity," he declared, "can be achieved only by a hierarchy of truths which show us which are fundamental and which subsidiary, which significant and which not."[5] As was the case fifty years later, critics who enjoyed fashioning themselves as political Leftists questioned such hierarchical thinking. Intellectual freedom implied no such hierarchy, though many such self-styled critics of the late twentieth century actually harbored yet more rigid hierarchies themselves, given the uncritical acceptance and elevation demanded of artifacts of cultures officially deemed "oppressed." In Hutchins' time the spectre of the fascists' repression of artists and intellectuals reinforced the criticism of any excessive rigidity with respect to culture from either political extreme. Hutchins and others could point out that the socialist ideals of much of the Left were proving to be no less repressive wherever they were instituted. Rationalizing their "middle," they could sincerely assert that total intellectual freedom was ultimately self-contradictory, and that their ideal held the fewest, though not an absence of, strictures.

Within the field of education many of the opponents of Hutchins considered themselves followers of John Dewey. The ideal of pragmatic educational training was construed to eschew impractical studies of Classical texts. With this came "relativist" rationale justifying negations or revisions of classical curricula. Dewey himself hardly praised those, notably at Columbia University's Teachers' College, who claimed to be following him. Indeed Dewey issued an important dictum about culture in the late 1930s. He wrote of a "kind of culture so free in itself that it conceives and begets political freedom as its accompaniment and consequences."[6] Dewey questioned whether such prescriptions as Hutchins' could readily promote this sort of culture.[7] Thus the two fought over means, but they were ultimately after the same end. Hutchins certainly

believed his curriculum would support the very culture Dewey envisaged. Similarly, enthusiasts in the mainstream of American culture like
Sinclair Lewis and John dos Passos did not feel themselves to be turn-
ing away from freedom as they shifted from the political left toward the
middle. Rather they saw themselves maximizing freedom in an admittedly imperfect world that was witnessing genuine violations of freedom
elsewhere. Many of the arts of the era indeed exemplified this allegedly conformist freedom—"to say what I had to say," as Aaron Copland
recalled, "in the simplest possible terms." The non-conformists and critics were not heeded and the mainstream comforted itself in the knowledge that America's political fringes, while largely ignored, were free to
speak and not be killed or sent to labor camps. The irony of this freedom to speak and be ignored would receive fuller development, not
coincidentally in more economically comfortable times.

In the thirties the pressures of Soviet and Nazi spectres gave
American freedom a negative definition and justification. Freedom
meant the lack of fascism or communism. After the defeat of fascism
the definition of freedom as that which was not communism grew to
greater proportions. During the WPA the Dies Commission had sought
to root out many allegedly dangerous left wing subversives from the
government arts programs. During the war some artists were employed
to make films and create posters for information, propaganda and morale
boosting. Here again some Congressional conservatives, uncomfortable
with the extent to which America's alliance with Russia could unduly
accommodate domestic leftists, maintained a wary watchfulness. This
concern grew after the war, most famously with the work of the House
Un-American Affairs Committee and the truculence of Senator Joseph
McCarthy. While State Department personnel and people in the entertainment business were the most known victims of these activities, the
arts continued to hold a place of suspicion in the minds of many right
wing members of Congress.

Through the late 1940s and into the 1950s the State Department quietly borrowed from private collections and on several occasions bought
paintings of various American artists. Their desire was to put works on
display, formally in showings or less formally in Embassies, thus using
the art as propaganda. The excellence of the work would serve as an
advertisement of the greatness of American culture to other nations for
whose affections and loyalty the U.S. was battling with the Soviet
Union. Further, some of the secured works were of modern abstract
expressionist styles. Some in the State Department felt they could exem-

plify the artistic freedom of America in contrast to the increasingly known horrors of Stalinism and the arts. Such modern works, however, were the very sort which raised the ire of conservative Congressional leaders. To many such officials, "modern art" was virtually synonymous with subversion and communism. Additionally modern art was regarded as antithetical to the decent, wholesome American traditions best displayed to the world. The moderns thus smacked of the worst form of effete New York City decadence as well as of communism. Indeed President Truman himself muttered: "so-called modern art is merely the vaporings of half-baked lazy people."[8]   His tastes ran to fellow Missourian Thomas Hart Benton.

Through the forties and fifties, a duality existed in the federal government with respect to the utility of the arts. The State Department was a leader in the idea that the arts constituted no threat and that, indeed, they could be readily marshalled in a cultural offensive that would be part of the overall propaganda battle against the Soviet Union. In opposition lay those who felt compelled to battle communism from within as well as without. In 1951 President Truman, aware of the cross currents here, requested a report on the state of the arts and government. The disharmony between the State Department and members of Congress could not be resolved by any sort of policy or fiat. It had to be left to the political tides. At first the conservatives in Congress were the stronger force. The work of HUAC and of McCarthy and his associates snuffed out any possibility of government involvement with individuals or organizations concerned with any such potentially dangerous activities as the arts. Through the late 40s and into the 50s many resolutions came forth, notably from Congressmen Jacob Javits of New York and Charles Howell of New Jersey, calling for Federal activism in the arts, largely via advisory commissions. The expenses in all such proposed cases would have been minimal. But they were all defeated. The opposition's arguments focused on the old themes of Jeffersonianism, Federalism, and budgetary concerns. These same arguments would later fail as the government increasingly accepted the legitimacy of activism. A key changed circumstance was that by the mid and late fifties the anti-communist hysteria had subsided and the arts in America had come to be seen as a part of the fight against communism. While no less immune than their right wing Congressional colleagues with respect to paranoia about communism, the State Department had shown less distaste with respect to the arts and their potentially positive relationship with the government. Perhaps because their concerns could not focus on domestic matters, they could not be so fully swept up by the hysteria surrounding HUAC and McCarthyism. In this regard, many involved in such domestic movements held, of course, that the State Department itself was full of subversives like Alger Hiss and Dean Acheson. The Department had to tread lightly, and their use of art for propaganda drew minor fire. Some voiced suspicions at the use of American artists, because of their alleged subversive intentions, in official efforts to display the cultural excellence and freedom of the nation. When the State Department began using art as anti-communist propaganda after World War II their efforts aroused suspicions. These suspicions remained but among an ever smaller audience through the 1950s. Such concerns of course insulted the intelligence of State Department officials, as, by implication, either the officials were themselves subversives or they had to be lacking in any ability to detect radical or subversive themes in a given work of art. Denial of subversive intent only confirmed it in the minds of McCarthyist Congressmen when facing artists. Such bludgeoning of officials from such offices as the State Department yielded diminishing success and increasing embarrassment to the political right. As crude McCarthyism increasingly proved to be anti-communism's worst domestic enemy, the role of the arts in the American political mainstream became a more positive one.

The State Department's sponsorship of a tour of American abstract expressionist painting in Latin America and Africa in 1955 provided a means of demonstrating yet another way in which America was superior and thus a better model for a Third World nation to follow. The hideous Stalinist oppression of artists, particularly of any who engaged in modern idioms like abstraction provided a strong propaganda opportunity. Few in Congress would deny the legitimacy of such a claim, or the righteousness in pressing its validity abroad. The positive place of the arts in a free America could now be asserted with greater safety. McCarthyist hysteria would continue to resonate in middle America and hold the arts suspect, and as long as such paranoia remained the place of the arts would have limits. Indeed the focus of the State Department was more political than artistic. The actual esthetic worth of such works was not the issue. Indeed the message was implicitly unsupportive or at least ambivalent in regard to the art itself. The State Department implicitly accepted the idea that this art was outrageous, the propaganda thus being in effect: We're so free we even put up with this.

Many artists involved in the abstract-expressionist movement—Jackson Pollock and Mark Rothko, for example—were hardly sympathetic with the goals of the State Department. Indeed the philosophical precepts of the movement were definitely at odds with the notion that their art could support any established political orthodoxy. This government "support" amounted to cooperation. To government officials and many supporters the tolerance of such arts was a genuine sign of the nation's political vitality, while to the artists it constituted a perfect example of what Herbert Marcuse later dubbed "repressive tolerance." With the attitudes of leaders like President Truman at best ambivalent to the esthetics of modern art and with the continued branding of many modernists as subversive, a safety zone found only in the propaganda mills of the State Department was not terribly comforting. The eclipsing of such Congressmen as Frederick Busby of Illinois and George Dondero of Michigan who had suspected Dean Acheson of being a communist was hardly a victory for the cause of the arts in America.

From the standpoint of American leaders, the country was locked into and obsessed with the fight against the Soviets for *world* hegemony. Thus any Gramscian-type arguments about an *esthetic* hegemony between the Congress and State Department was, even if understood, of little importance. The battle against the communists pervaded everything. Indeed in the mid 50s, with Sputnik and other events, the battle seemed possibly lost. The use of the arts for frankly propaganda purposes appeared in no way contradictory to the principle of liberty, any more than did Robert Hutchins' curricular hierarchies endanger freedom during the struggles against totalitarianism in the 1930s. Just as those who criticized Hutchins from the Left were often discounted in the 30s, those who saw repression in the political exploitation of the tolerance of modern art in the 50s were marginalized as quantitatively insignificant, a relegation which was another part of their repression.

In this very era of Eisenhower calm some intellectual leaders of the nation were giving rationalization to the notion of the vitality of the American political mainstream. In contrast to earlier Progressive historians, commentators like Louis Hartz and Daniel Boorstin saw the political center as sufficiently accommodating to the major political divisions so that meaningful discourse could occur without fundamental challenges to the structural norms of political power. Richard Hofstadter reinforced this theme in his famous *Age of Reform* when he held that many of the forces which have lain outside the vital center were best understood in terms of their sociological, psychological or even spiritual deficits. The implications of such views countered Gramscian concerns about hegemony. With respect to the American arts many of the outwardly strange modern idioms could then be seen as just that—strange, aberrational. The mainstream of art—the Americana scenes of Thomas Hart Benton, the ballets of Aaron Copland, the plays of Thornton Wilder—revealed the nations solidity. There was nothing strange or aberrational about such art, and the artists were certainly not communists. Such perspective grew in the fifties and displaced the hysteria while maintaining and extending the anti-communism that proceeded it. Only the tonality had changed.

To the degree that artistic, esthetic and political precepts were violated or ignored, the use of art for propaganda purposes in such an agency as the State Department had inherently subversive qualities. Here lay, and lies, an essential problem with the arts' linkage to government. As the government is an inescapably political body, the arts' involvement with it invariably grows politicized. With subsuming Jeffersonian credo, many nineteenth-century politicians understood this and debated the legitimacy of the government being involved in any such endeavors as the arts and sciences. They were less concerned with contaminating art and science than with contaminating government. Jeffersonianism held that any such political involvement would be injurious to liberty. Pressing circumstances which, for example, led to the hiring of artists to design and decorate government buildings and to the significant funding of scientific research during the Civil War, revised this dogma but with respect to very specific goals. Generally the Jeffersonian wisdom dominated through the century, or, in contrast, perhaps an inherently anti-intellectual disdain for the arts and for the life of the mind gained support through a cynical use of a Jeffersonian vocabulary, galvanizing policies to which Jefferson himself would have taken exception. Whether the reasons were politically affirming or merely cynical, a pattern of neglect dominated the nineteenth century.

In the early twentieth century, as the purview of government grew and international image became increasingly important to many American leaders, needs arose for more permanent services from the government including artistic ones. But the activities of such permanent bodies as the National Commission of Fine Arts were then, and continue to be, matters of prescribed artistic service—a monument, a memorial, this building, etc. Such services were and, to some degree perhaps, remain the limits to which Federal sponsorship of the arts can go before vigorous controversy sets in. (And controversies have certainly come forth within the limited context of the National Commission anyway.) Even in such a narrow context art in itself remains largely untouched within political debates, and most initiatives devoted in some measure to the public support of art for art's sake failed until the New Deal. It was in the New Deal that the contrast between artistic service and *l'art pour l'art* grew visible. Sincere artists needed support, accepted it, but chafed under the strictures of government regulations which dictated proper topics of artistic focus, proper modes of expression, and even hours of labor. The desultory, artless nature of much of this bureaucracy grew increasingly apparent to many involved artists. Surrounding were Congressional fears of Left-wing subversion. With the Cold War propaganda efforts supporting American arts led to a perceived co-optation of concepts of artistic freedom for the purpose of furthering a fight against a communist enemy.

A component of the self-satisfied assertions of the nationalistic theorists of the 1950s like Hartz and Boorstin held that the wisdom of the American political center lay in its tendency not to make major metaphysical shifts. One of the salient features of the arts and their history is that they thrive on seeking and making such shifts all the time. Like a comet and a planet the arts and the American political mainstream rarely align. Any attempt to compel an alignment will reduce the inherent qualities of one if not both. But the mutually supporting championing of consensus politics and anti-communism dominated at this time. This brought the arts out of the shadow of McCarthyism but placed them under more subtle constrictions. Through the decade the arts then remained suspect to some politicians, a useful propaganda item to others. The esthetic autonomy of art was under pressure in either case. The State Department could use art, but the majority of Congress continued to block any official supportive or advisory measures, though the number of the sympathetic was rising. With that one element of hope, in the 1950s it remained a question whether the government could actually support art as art.

The Cold War had permanently altered the political spectrum of America. Before World War II the political right had always held to the wisdom of minimal government. Over the years elements of hypocrisy were certainly present, with, for example, the platitudes of laissez-faire masking government favors continually handed out to business, and with business regulations regularly subverted to the interests of those businesses in question. But after 1945 government could not remain even nominally minimal. The perceived threat of communism required the maintenance of virtual wartime levels of military expenditures. With military expenditures and general Cold War sensibilities, many other government activities won the support of conservatives, all to the steady erosion of traditional Jeffersonian conservatism. Enormous expenditures in education and science, highly motivated by concerns about Russian prowess grew throughout the fifties. In the year after Sputnik I, Congress tripled the National Science Foundation budget, passed the National Defense Education Act, and created the National Aeronautics Space Administration. Such expenditures logically prompted arguments promoting a widening of the government's purview here. If the government was concerned with the development of scientific education among America's youth, other components of intellectual development could not be neglected either. Similarly, if international prestige in science was a legitimate motive for government activism, other genres should be promoted as well. An Eisenhower administration report declared "a high civilization must not limit its efforts to science alone," and in 1955 the President in his State of the Union Address called for a Federal Advisory Commission on the Arts.[9]

Traditional culture had come a long way since the heyday of HUAC and McCarthy. At Eisenhower's first inauguration some music written by the composer Aaron Copland was scrapped from the program. Like many of his generation Copland had had a mild flirtation with the political left in the early 30s, and the new administration's leadership did not want to make even the slightest error to upset the far right. By the mid and late fifties this political wing had spent itself. The Eisenhower administration could verbally support the value of the arts in society without political risk. Bills supportive of the arts would continue to die, however, as Republicans and Southern Democrats mouthed states rights platitudes and voiced budgetary concerns.

The growing perception of the positive role culture could have on behalf of freedom amidst the Cold War came forth most starkly in 1958 when the Texas-born pianist Van Cliburn won the Tchaikovsky Piano Competition in Moscow. Cliburn's triumph came but six months after the Russians' successful launching of the Sputnik satellite. The State Department had expressed strategic interest in promoting Americans to excel in such international arts competitions. This was part of their overall propaganda campaign with the arts. In 1952 they quietly prompted the Ford Foundation to subvene expenses of Americans at the Queen Elizabeth Competition in Brussels. That year their sponsored competitor, Leon Fleisher, won first prize. In 1954 Eisenhower began a Program for Cultural Presentations Abroad, spending over $16 million from 1955 to 1961. While these cultural efforts and competitions were generally side shows, with Van Cliburn the State Department's sensitivity to international prestige in the arts proved to have more than a minor resonation among the American public. The Russians had remained preeminent in concert music with the prestige of such composers as Dimitri Shostakovich, Aram Katchaturian, and Serge Prokofiev (who had moved to the West with the Revolution but had later moved back to Russia). While critics had wrestled with the idea that such excellence came in spite of the Soviet system, the Soviets' status here remained undeniable. Among Americans' many counterpoints here was the assertion that while Russian music may be excellent, American technology and science were the world's finest. Thus when Sputnik was launched, American technology was embarrassed, so when Cliburn soon thereafter beat the Soviets at what we begrudgingly admitted they did best, the reaction was colossal. Americans seized upon Van Cliburn with an adulation that eclipsed any given to a concert musician before or since. With Mayor Robert Wagner officially declaring Van Cliburn Day, the pianist received a ticker tape in New York that rivaled those of Charles Lindbergh and Amelia Earhart. At a similar celebration in Philadelphia crowds tore at his limousine. For over a year mob scenes erupted wherever Cliburn went shopping. Young women screamed at his concerts. The Chicago Elvis Presley Fan Club renamed itself the Van Cliburn Fan Club. Cliburn appeared on several television shows—"What's My Line," Steve Allen, and Edward R. Murrow's "Person to Person"—and he was given an official reception at the White House.

Cliburn's career reached enormous, and perhaps unjustifiable heights as a consequence of the fortuitous timing of the Moscow triumph. Critics have noted the pianist's narrowness of repertory, focusing on the very Romantic/Russian traditions on which the Tchaikovsky Competition centers. They see his extreme fussiness in endlessly recording and re-recording indicate a certain lack of self-confidence and yielding performances akin to drawings with countless erasures and corrections. Artists normally have the right to withhold a recording from release, and at RCA Van Cliburn has more such withholdings than any other musician. The habitual slowness of Cliburn's tempi in so many of his interpretations, while suited to his beloved Russian Romantics, indicates a lack of artistic breadth. Critic Joseph Horowitz noted Cliburn's "lustrous sheen and monumental architecture attain a sort of embalmed perfection."[10] Borrowing from the title of a popular Broadway play of the day, *New York Times Magazine* writer Abram Chasins entitled an article: "Will Success Spoil Van Cliburn?" Most have come to believe it did.

He luxuriated in the success achieved at the age of twenty-three. But artistic growth from that point is hard to detect. After 1978 Cliburn went into virtual retirement. Were critics and historians to name the world's top fifty pianists of the latter half of the twentieth century Cliburn would certainly be on most lists, but he would not stand head and shoulders above the field as did such artists of previous times as Franz Liszt, Joseph Hoffmann, Arthur Schnabel, Arthur Rubenstein, Vladimir Horowitz and Rudolph Serkin, nor does he perhaps quite stand with such roughly contemporary figures as Claudio Arrau, Glenn Gould or Vladimir Aschkenazy.

Historians have concluded that during Khurshchev's regime the Russians considerable achievements in space technology stemmed less from the society's overall economic and technological strength and more from the intentional funnelling of valuable resources to particular, often flashy, ends like sports, rockets, the military, and the arts. All this contributed to the nation's more general impoverishment. By choice and proclivity, Cliburn too had narrowed his own artistic resources to the particular repertorial dictates of one competition. He achieved success but thereafter appeared as much suffused as elevated by the triumph. And as others shot past him with wider technical possibilities his triumph seemed as much a curio of a particular political age as a launching of any new artistic one. In that regard Cliburn was very much an American Sputnik.

Cliburn's triumph did indicate a lingering strain of inferiority in some Americans' cultural self image in 1958. Feeling in competition with the Russians in all spheres of life, Americans recognized their shortcomings, some of which lay in traditional high culture. Prior generations had revealed such senses of inferiority but often responded with a smug, populist anti-intellectualism or by finding comfort in Jefferson's view that any such impoverishment was a price well worth paying in order to avoid European corruption. While such non-entangling and populist sensibilities remained, in the Cold War they were eclipsed by a belief that America had inherited the mantle of free world leadership and thus needed to correct any points of possible international embarrassment. One key to Cliburn's immense popularity here lay in the way his personality and style embodied many of the traditional isolationist/populist sensibilities, while his musicianship met the cultural exigencies of the Cold War, a perfect combination of unassuming charm and classical artistry. Cliburn delighted television audiences with his ease with trivial talk show banter (which was all new then). He never appeared aloof

or condescending. His lanky, at times almost awkward Texas manner
was as much a hit as his music. Cliburn's teacher at the Julliard School,
Rosina Lhevinne, herself a Russian emigre and a distinguished graduate
of the Kiev Conservatory, encountered Cliburn's Texas roots whey they
met. His first words to her were allegedly: "Honey, ah'm 'on study with
you.'" Whether true or not, the quotation caught on in the press, literally and figuratively playing well in Peoria. Vernacular and high culture
had been so often at odds in American history. Though each's snobbish
proponents would rarely admit it, they admired one another's qualities—
the mass popularity of the vernacular; the technical mastery of classical
artists. Revealing of this admiration was the way the two came together with Van Cliburn.

Of further delight to middle America were reports of the pianist's
statements and misstatements while in Russia. To Nikita Khrushchev's
grinning inquiry about why he was so tall, the lanky Cliburn drawled:
"cause Ah'm from Texas." Populist America enjoyed Cliburn's inadvertent flub at a reception where he mistakenly addressed Khrushchev's
political rival Nikolai Bulganin as "Mr. Molotov." Khrushchev had just
ousted Molotov and was about to do the same to Bulganin, so the equally populist Ukranian peasant likely enjoyed the gaffe even more.

While snippets of American populism and Western Classicism could
combine readily with Van Cliburn, the contrast between them continued
to be evident to Americans who thought seriously about the nation's
place in the world of culture. In some genres of popular culture achievements were considerable. In certain traditional high culture genres
shortcomings continued to embarrass. Many anti-elite elitists respond,
then and since, with apathy, but amidst the international rivalries of the
1950s potential and real cultural embarrassments appeared to affect the
country in many contexts. The arts were but one issue. Sports too were
an area in which the Soviets sought to upstage Americans. In response
to this challenge the government promoted physical fitness in schools to
beat the Russians just as it was nurturing science. In 1955
Representative Frank Thompson of New Jersey proposed a National Art,
Sports and Recreation Bill for this purpose. Budgetary and states' rights
arguments killed it.

In regard to the city of Washington, D.C. there emerged a growing
sense of the town being culturally backward. An official hardship post
to many foreign diplomats in much of the nineteenth century, problems
of malaria, typhus and yellow fever had passed, but the continuing
plagues of segregation, racism and poverty were still very much on

hand. Just as the State Department had nudged the Ford Foundation to assist Americans in international arts competitions, they presented a friend-of-the-court brief to the Supreme Court with respect to the Brown v. Board of Education case of 1954, alerting the Court that America's international standing was injured by foreigners encounters with Jim Crow. Segregation's visibility in the nation's capital underscored this especially. With such motives the Federal government began some sorely needed renewal projects. Not all were successful.

A paradox here lay in the cultural roots of such idioms as jazz, blues, and rock and roll often emanating from these poorer communities. African American artists like Louis Armstrong and Count Basie, who grew up amidst poverty and segregation were proving to be some of the country's most powerful cultural ambassadors. Well meaning leaders thus wished to eradicate many of the oppressive conditions from which such cultures had arisen. A very tricky balancing act here tested the sensitivity of any involved.

Another anomaly lay in the fact that many Cold War cultural leaders desired an elevation of the elite culture at least superficially bound to the classes responsible for or blithely ignorant of the oppression of many poor. Counterfactually, the Soviets indeed lionized American jazz and allowed recordings and concerts to tour all over the country not merely because the music was esthetically appealing (artistic excellence was certainly never an effective shield against repression there) but because jazz could underscore the racism they wished to characterize as endemic to the enemy's society. Amidst such cultural offensives and counteroffensives, a key then would be for American officials to find and develop a culture that could encompass a breadth of social components or to administer an institution that could accommodate the diverse elements and let each shine on its own.

In the late 1950s and early 60s, at the same time embarrassment was growing over the visible state of poverty in Washington, concerns grew about the city being a hick town with respect to culture. Museums were plentiful, but symphony, opera, ballet, theatre and other genres were sadly lacking in comparison to the world's other major capitals. To this end, in 1958 President Eisenhower signed a law to create a National Center for the Performing Arts in Washington. This would eventually be the Kennedy Center for the Performing Arts. With the glitz of the Kennedy administration increasing numbers of people motivated to establish more than a mere facade of internationally renowned American culture, for Washington as well as for the nation as a whole. During the

Kennedy administration the Camelot image and the dictates of the Cold War readily meshed. Edward R. Murrow, Kennedy's Director of the United States Information Agency, wrote to the Senate Committee on Labor and Public Welfare that there was a "Communist Cultural Offensive" with which the United States must contend. In international cultural activity the Soviets, he claimed, were continuing to outperform the United States. America's populist cultural provincialism seemed an isolationist indulgence no longer affordable.[11]

Back in the nineteenth century many prominent Americans had noted the low international status of American culture and proposed various measures to the government to correct this state of affairs. But they were not heeded. Amidst Camelot and the Cold War the same expressions came to have fuller resonance. In 1961 the Metropolitan Opera Company went on strike. President Kennedy appointed future Supreme Court Justice Arthur Goldberg to mediate. Such a step itself indicated at least a greater rhetorical concern the Kennedy administration would have for the arts. Goldberg found that the wage demands of labor were legitimate but that these demands, if met, would force such high ticket prices to cover the costs that either the art would be available to but the very rich or the Company would go bankrupt. Bankruptcy would hurt in the culture wars with the Soviets, whose opera and ballets enjoyed great prestige. Federal activism was seen as a viable mechanism here to prevent both the financial ruin or the elite domination of the arts.[12]

In 1962 Kennedy appointed a Presidential Advisory Council on the Arts, under August Heckscher, an editorial writer with the moderately conservative *New York Herald Tribune.* Heckscher was less enthusiastic than many in the Kennedy administration concerning the results of government activism in the arts. The President may have felt that the appointment of such a moderate as Heckscher would lend greater weight to any recommendations. In his report Heckscher asserted that an appreciation of the arts required the knowledge and vision of the spectator. If that was lacking, he implied, government support could be dragged down by a crass democratization. Thus, he asserted, "when government has entered directly into the field of art, the experience too often has been disheartening." Noting that success has occurred when the government has been involved in scientific fields, however, Heckscher did not recommend inaction but noted caution. He saw government particularly able to promote art education to the young and to support new developments in the arts which mainstream institutions tend to avoid. In 1963 Heckscher recommended the establishment of an Advisory

Council on the Arts and of a National Arts Foundation to judge and administer grants. In June, 1963, Kennedy established an Advisory Council; he died before it met, however. Upon taking office, Lyndon Johnson would be less circumspect. President Johnson would replace Heckscher with Roger Stevens, Chair of the Kennedy Center of the Performing Arts, a man much more bold in regard to the question of what government could do in the arts. Stevens would become the first Chairman of the National Endowment for the Arts.

In October, 1963 the Senate held hearings on the idea of creating a national arts foundation. Such suggestions had come forth during the Eisenhower years. They had been voted down, but each time support increased. This time scores of experts testified, as did many prominent Congressmen and Senators themselves. Almost all favored passage of some sort of endowment. In their collective statements they encapsulated the various viewpoints which had supported government activism in the arts since the days of John Quincy Adams, as well as echoing the Cold War sensibilities which had come to have application to the arts: The arts perpetuate and enliven enduring humanistic values. Other nations of equal stature, as well as many of lower international standing, engage in such activism. Such government activism is indicative of a mature nation and culture to which third world nations will look with admiration. The nation already devotes public resources to the sciences, so the arts and humanities deserve some support too. The government support can lend the arts levels of reification, an ever pressing need amidst the social alienation and accompanying artistic abstraction of the day. The American people find themselves with steadily increasing leisure time, the positive use of which the government ought foster. Certain states were already engaging in such activities with general success, notably New York which began in 1961. The quality of Americans' performance in the arts is one of many genres of human activity in which we are competing with the Soviet Union for the hearts and minds of people throughout the world, and is one where we currently risk falling short, as Sputnik revealed with respect to science and technology.[13] The tone of the hearings was not one of despair but of can-do optimism. Still, with financial concerns and a related philosophy distrustful of government activism remaining strong, the hearings yielded no successful legislation during the Kennedy administration.

A month after the hearings President Kennedy died. Much of the cultural glitz that surrounded his administration appeared to dim with the more earthy Lyndon Johnson. While the Kennedys' had entertained, for example, such musical guests as Pablo Cassals and Leonard Bernstein, under President Johnson the first White House musical performance was a hootenanny. But such changes of tone did not fundamentally alter the continuing desire for activism by the government in the arts and elsewhere. Indeed in practical legislative terms Johnson was much more successful than Kennedy. In the months before his death, Kennedy's momentum with Congress seemed virtually at a halt. For several reasons Johnson was able to regenerate this. Kennedy's death itself served as an impetus for much legislation passing in memorium. The National Culture Center, originally proposed by J. William Fulbright in 1958, was renamed after the slain President. In regard to the successful legislation in the first two years of Johnson's Presidency, much has also been made of Johnson's jawboning and keen cloak-room political skills. While such skills were undeniable, Johnson also had the benefit of the Congress elected with him in 1964 being much more supportive. Among the dizzying array of legislation then passed in 1965 were the Elementary and Secondary Education Act which, under Titles I and III, promoted schools to develop programs which incorporated arts and cultural sources, and the National Foundation on the Arts and Humanities Act, which created the National Endowments for the Arts and the Humanities.

In 1964 a government report came forth from the combined efforts of the American Council of Learned Societies, the Council of Graduate Schools, and the United Chapters of Phi Beta Kappa. The report stressed similar themes as had those who testified before the Senate the year before, emphasizing particularly the embarrassing state of American culture *vis à vis* that of other nations over whom the country postures leadership. How could the world's best hope, a Great Society, have such a lowly culture? Cold War fears and shibboleths did not take up much wording, likely not for those sensibilities fading but for their being so uncritically ensconced in the political mainstream that any mention of "international standing" covered the matter. Amidst the grieving over Kennedy and the Great Society momentum which earmarked Johnson's honeymoon period with Congress, the *Report* appeared to resonate deeply.

The fear of second-class status in culture hailed memories of the Sputnik anxieties. In this regard the *Report* held that the science crisis had passed and asserted that now the same could be done with respect to the Arts and Humanities. The emphasis on science in government, as well as in general education spending in the late 1950s and early 60s had created an imbalance between these intellectual areas. Proponents of funding the arts and humanities voiced this sentiment as much as any in 1964 and 1965. Congressman Adam Clayton Powell of New York bemused that if Socrates were an American citizen in 1965 he would be working for the National Institute of Mental Health. Senator Edward Kennedy of Massachusetts noted that all American advances in science and technology would prove of little value in international opinion without accompanying advances in the arts, without which we would be seen as "dull and listless men."[14] Cold War thinking remained at root amidst such sentiments. Arts and Humanities support following the aid to science trained the whole mind and engaged the international battle on all fronts. With the creation of the Arts and Humanities Endowments the place of government in the arts assumed one akin to those of most developed nations, at least structurally.

The nature of the American political culture which so long resisted government activism in the arts would continue to be very much in evidence whenever the topic of government and the arts received attention during times of Congressional refunding, as well as in a more general setting. A chief problem over the years of the Endowments has involved the appearance of their susceptibility to political pressures which cloud purely artistic, educational and scholarly concerns. When in power the political right has been accused of promoting largely mainstream culture and values and negating the artistic outcroppings of economically marginal cultures and of the avant garde. Conversely the left of the political center has been in control of the Endowments at various times, and they have been charged with ignoring the artistic mainstream and elevating the "margins" beyond their inherent artistic worth, and often as pawns in a clumsily played game of sociological chess, allegedly proving a strident closed-mindedness in stark contrast to the projected self-image of openness. Such left-of-center sentiments are also charged to lie within the staff of the Endowments, allegedly then subverting the desires of more right-wing officials placed at various times at the top of the Endowments' structure. Most famous have also been accusations of improper and unnecessary support of elements of the avant-garde whose *raison d'etre* has allegedly involved more the intentional shocking of audiences than the development of any particular esthetic precept. The Endowment's officials, Congress, the press and the public at large have grappled with these charges. No resolutions have come forth, nor will they to the satisfaction of most, let alone all interested parties. The emotional stakes are often high, to the point of transcending the esthetic questions at hand.

When the Endowments first began under Lyndon Johnson the optimism of the Great Society was pervasive. The largesse of the government would provide not merely the financial but the structural basis for a more uniform and harmonious society that would actually eliminate poverty, alienation and injustice. Cynical hindsight may snicker at such sensibilities. Right wing analysts see it as constituting a form of original sin with respect to the stimulation of massive and wasteful bureaucracies. But Johnson and many of his supporters honestly believed in such ideals. Acknowledging the lack of success here, historians remain divided over whether such ideals were utterly misguided, whether government bureaucracies could actually change the patterns of racism and poverty, elitism and alienation, whether greater progress would have occurred but for the quagmire of Vietnam sucking necessary funding out of the programs just as they were beginning to work, or whether subsequent administrations failed to follow the still open directions of the Great Society.

With the New Deal some historians have argued that in FDR's programs there never existed any utopian dream to be betrayed in the first place.[15] In their desultory, often pedestrian nature some WPA programs reflected this, to the disappointment of many participants. Within the Great Society, however, such dreams were real, if only fleeting. As part of the Great Society goal of a perfected nation, the Arts and Humanities Endowments were to foster a truly national culture, eclipsing such old barriers as class, race, gender and region. Yet during the decades of government activism in the arts and humanities a national culture has not emerged. Some would argue that the culture has grown more divisive.

The largesse of the Endowments has rendered American culture more varied by the promotion of the visibility of many theretofore obscure pockets of culture as well as in the support of the institutional mainstream of American arts and letters. Before the National Endowment for the Humanities the major research institutions in the humanities were small in number and, in effect, comprised a rather exclusive club. This state has loosened in the last third of the twentieth century, and the NEH has played a major role in this as it has opened possibilities for many institutions of formerly marginal status with respect to research. To some critics this has gone too far, unjustifiably prompting lesser schools to emphasize research, to open graduate-level programs, and to seek support for areas of educational activism for which they are not equipped, all to the detriment of equally valuable educational functions like instruction for which they are better suited. The role of politics enters here as Congressmen and Senators press for Endowment dollars to flow into institutions in their districts, and some Presidentially appointed Arts and Humanities Council members and administrators advocate regional sensitivity in the dispersal of funds.

The funding of mainstream institutions in the arts has been a major function of the National Endowment for the Arts in its first twenty-five years. This has not been done just by specific design, for the Endowment has often tried to support diverse styles, genres and institutions. But the pattern of support to the mainstream has emerged as a result of the preponderance of the Gifts in Matching as the method of dispersing funds. Under Richard Nixon the Endowments' allocations rose from $10 million to over $20 million each. Many new programs thus began or greatly expanded—the Jazz Program, the Artists-in-Schools Program, the Orchestra Program, the Museum Program. Much of the sizable increase under Nixon focused on matching funds. Many distinctions between the United States' and other nations' support of the arts show the U.S. to be less involved. A strong mitigating factor here lies in the U.S. government allowing deductions from taxable personal and corporate incomes for contributions to the arts as charitable institutions. This is not the case in Germany, France or England. Thus while the government of then West Germany in 1988 outspent the U.S. government by 400% in the arts (not merely per capita but in total), the government-encouraged private donations in the U.S. render the contrast less stark. No figures exist to show how much Americans would give to the arts were it not for tax breaks, but it is no great risk to assert that the deductions are an enormous inducement to Americans' support here. The recognition of this led the Endowment's leaders to see an emphasis on matching gifts as an effective mechanism, thus also placing an unmistakably American stamp of entrepreneurialism on the way the nation supports its culture.

The emphasis on matching awards can be criticized for rewarding the artistic mainstream, for those sectors of the arts tend to have the strongest connections to the corporate world. The assumption in such criticism tends to be that corporate support, as in politics, tends to favor conservative esthetics. Some validity certainly exists in such claims. In music, particularly, corporate sponsorship has been most generous with symphony orchestras and opera companies who focus on the standard 1750-1920 literature and rarely perform any work written after 1945. Even government grants to musical organizations for performances of "new" music have tended to support, via the paying of hefty copyright fees to publishers, modern composers like Copland, Thomson, Katchaturian, and Prokofiev, who have written in accessible, nineteenth-century Romantic forms and harmonies. Accentuating this point, one more modern composer—John Adams—received substantial support via the Houston Opera for his thematically and harmonically accessible work Nixon in China. Rarely do orchestras and opera houses perform works written in modern, dissonant languages, and when they do ticket purchases and charitable support (hence matching money) tends to fall off. In the early 1970s, for example, the Buffalo Philharmonic employed the modernist composer/conductor Lukas Foss as their music director. Foss performed a steady stream of works by such moderns as Pierre Boulez, Karl Stockhausen and himself. Ticket sales, contributions, and orchestra morale all fell off. Michael Tilson Thomas replaced him in 1972. He gave greater emphasis to the Classical/Romantic/Impressionist literature. Morale, ticket sales and contributions all rose again. Both Foss and Thomas are first-rank musicians, so quality was not a mitigating factor here. It solely was a matter of esthetics and repertory.

The conservative tendencies in orchestras and opera houses are less severe with respect to other musical genres—small ensembles, chamber works, musicals—although with musicals the harmonic language tends not to engage the esthetic controversies which distinguish "modern" from "standard" symphonic music. And with musicals, not coincidentally, popular support does not wane so sharply with respect to anything new, so much so indeed that the institutions staging musicals have not needed or sought as much public funding, as have the more traditional, rarefied genres. Justifications for supporting such accessible art forms have followed the line that the public, particularly the youth, gains from exposure to such art. Phenomenology then dictates that public taste must be acknowledged and not high-handedly bypassed. So any excessive commerce with styles apt to shock or unduly confront sensibilities is avoided.

In the visual arts much modern abstract art has tended to gain more support, both corporate and public, than have its counterparts in music. Still, there have been substantial controversies surrounding the modern visual arts, generating heated political debates, at times leading to a fall off of support for modern idioms. Defenders of the moderns have tended to criticize such mainstream tendencies, but they have risked falling into the trap of uncritical self-promotion. Artists readily assert their status as avant-gardists, but their assertion is not proof, and defenses against criticism easily lapse into summary dismissals of critics with the same high handedness they criticize many esthetic conservatives for employing against the avant garde. Such a skewed state of art/criticism communication makes judgments difficult. A rejoinder of "why judge?" would be logical except for the fact that choices in the allocations of public funds are at stake. Thus all contending sides cannot avoid struggle.

One reason for the funding of modern visual art more than modern music involves the fact that with music the majority of public money goes to the performing organization which, in turn, awards artists who have created the work to be performed. Less often have public funds gone directly to composers, as in past times private grants fell to a Mozart or Beethoven, simply to write a piece of music. The same was the case during the New Deal when the Federal Music Project never sponsored the writing of a new composition. The nature of the musical art form, with the performance or recording, as opposed to the completed score, being more the actual art, renders such a structure fitting. In other arts, particularly the visual, the created work is "consumed" with less such a significant intermediary as an orchestra or performer on hand. Granted, the display area or museum provides some esthetic backdrop and influence, but the importance is hardly the same as that of a performer with respect to a piece of music.

Orchestras and other performance organizations have logically tended to be the institutions through which many grants for compositions have been generated. Some theatres and museums have been awarded Endowment grants to turn over to specific artists. In the arts and humanities such practices have engendered questions as to whether the process inadvertently winnows precious funds through extra bureaucratic labyrinths which absorb some of the money for administrative overhead. While an orchestra is hardly such a needless filter, others legally constituted do indeed draw off resources. Colleges and universities, for example, tend to administer the grants secured by various professors in various arts and humanities disciplines. These institutions normally tack a percentage onto the grant's budget to cover their administrative costs. The percentage normally runs around forty, though some go much higher. In 1991 Stanford University was exposed for having generally inflated science, arts, and humanities grants by an average of seventy percent and placed much of the extra funds into general campus maintenance and supply. The school was quite embarrassed by the exposure of administrative overhead on grants being used to maintain a university-owned yacht and to furnish its president's home with lavish ornaments.

The Endowments have not been the ones who have let this occur, for the screening of expenditures is not their legally constituted function. Further, the "indirect cost" percentage charged to the government is legal. It is a product of negotiations between the individual institution and the General Accounting Office. Whatever figure those two parties agree upon the Endowments must accept.

The Endowments have to some degree attempted to shy away from "regrants" to other institutions who in turn judge and award grants to curb at least the appearance of thickening bureaucracies. While seeking to emphasize direct grants and matching, the Endowments encourage certain approaches and strategies inherent in the fields at hand. The matching fund emphases, in addition to promoting the mainstream art which the corporate world tends to favor, tends also to reward the more entrepreneurial applicant/recipient. This can be criticized as well as defended. The criticism is that such entrepreneurial skills are not analogous to the creative and intellectual skills to be promoted by the Endowments. Indeed such business acumen can be seen as contradictory to artistic talent, given the well-known business ineptness of many past artistic and scientific geniuses. (Imagine, such an argument could conjecture, asking Albert Einstein to scour for matching funds to secure a grant from the National Science Foundation.) While it is at least fashionable for many artists to cast themselves as such, more likely the two skills are mutually exclusive with respect to the personalities of people who have received grants. It is simply fun for some artists, when turned down for grants, to engage in corporate and government bashing and to posture their lack of entrepreneurialism as proof of their artistic quality. Further, a general entrepreneurial sense is not independent of the skills of "grantsmanship" that play a part in the mechanics of public awards. So any removal of corporate connections would not necessarily remove the entrepreneurial factor in the allocation of arts and humanities grants anyway. It would but slightly alter the requisite bureaucratic "language" skills. The image of the noble artist best left autonomous is largely historical fiction. Virtually all artists have had to petition available institutions—the Church, the aristocracy, the business community, the government. Many famous stories like that of Mozart vs. Salieri center on those who failed to gain support in their time while others, whom posterity clearly judges to have been inferior, fared nicely. People's desire to see power fail renders stories of Mozart's struggles more compelling than those of Haydn's contentment. With respect to any such failures, the problem is that no system has ever adequately replaced "the marketplace of ideas" within governments or in the private sectors concerning what makes great art or scholarship. For whatever systems are erected, be they explicit and public or implicit and private, they yield a scramble for resources and ultimately imprecise human judgments entering into their allocations. Thus those who criticize the means of allocation, even if successful in changing them, tend to create no more just a system but only a replacement. In any era some artistic mediocrities gain more acclaim than others recognized as geniuses. The artist who is philosophically consistent and pure tends to ignore such concerns, create on his or her own, and have no truck with the games of funding. And indeed a few late twentieth-century artists who have criticized the alleged Victorianism of the National Endowment for the Arts have no link to organizations which have vied for funding. Others are not so pure.

Where there is funding there must be decisions. Where there are decisions there must be guidelines, standards and judgments. Focusing on the art and scholarship which the Endowments support, the overwhelming standard has been quality. Only at the fringes has there been controversy. Within the Arts and Humanities Endowments have come various emphases as administrations have come and gone. During the Carter Administration came a decided emphasis on education programs, scholarship and arts which enhanced the status and visibility of women and minorities. In the Reagan and Bush years some, though not all such emphases continued. In the Humanities Endowment the Reagan years saw some self-imposed spending cuts under the Chairmanship of William Bennett, the first significant cut (twenty-five percent) since the Endowment's beginning.

Under Bennett's successor Lynne Cheney there emerged an explicit de-emphasis of certain "modern" theories, growing in many humanities disciplines, generally cast under the loose labels of semiotics and deconstruction. The debate over this rattled about the Academy and pertinent private and public funding agencies. Critics of the exclusion consider it an unjust casting off of an entire scholarly approach which has intrinsic merit. The policy's defenders consider deconstruction an intellectual *cul de sac*, replete with mindless disciples more enamored of obscuring a topic or text at hand with jargon than of enlivening it with analysis, a kind of literary junk bond contributing nothing to the content of the text at hand, diverting potentially beneficial analytical resources onto levels which provide but illusory and banal psychic pleasure. Such potential problems of discipledom are present with respect to any analytical mode in the Academy. With deconstruction, the adolescent narrowness of the approach renders the legitimate not easily separable from the vapid. Hence, critics argue, let the marketplace of ideas work for a time and settle the matter more before public funds be allocated. Meanwhile the absence of public funds need not deny the approach. The funds are not entitlements. All citizens are entitled but to apply for funds. The government is under no obligation to fund all genres of scholarship in the Academy.

The controversy over deconstruction has been significant within certain bounds of the academic world, but this has been minor compared to the furor over the Arts Endowment's alleged support of works some consider obscene. The issue here falls into two basic categories. One of the troublesome, recurring patterns in the public, as well as the private discussions of the issue has involved a continuous, unsystematic blending of these two. The first category involves the thorny questions of definition—what is art, and what is obscenity? The second category concerns what kinds of art should the government sponsor. Each question can be complicated; the morass is needlessly thickened by their unnecessary confusion. Certainly the points overlap, but the discourse over the issue could be rendered less rhetorically intense if the distinction were understood and handled with conceptual precision. This assumes, of course, a reduction in rhetorical heat is a desired result among interested parties. This may not be the case.

The question of what is art is in effect bounded by the question of what is obscene, and vice versa. Various societies have supported and defined art as creative work which reinforces individual and collective senses of what is beautiful and true, i.e., esthetic and ethical values. They have also accepted as art that which challenges and alters those same values. In regard to the "reinforcing" art, a boundary exists, explicitly or implicitly, beyond which lies mere propaganda or advertisement. Is the famous World War I recruitment poster—"Uncle Sam Wants You!"—a work of art? Such an issue goes to the question of where that boundary lies. Indeed some of Andy Warhol's activity—for example, the Campbell's Soup Cans and the Marilyn Monroe works—hold intellectual interest for their engaging that very issue. While Warhol has ultimately fallen into the art category, debate can still be broached here, and the question continues. Is the music of a TV advertisement genuinely art? Such a question is left to the marketplace of ideas, and calmly so because the stakes of public concern seem not terribly high. While the stakes are low regarding art and propaganda; they have tended to be higher with respect to the definition of obscenity. Art which successfully challenges individual and collective senses of truth, beauty and goodness often achieves historic greatness, for it contributes to the formation of new paradigms and allows civilizations to evolve (or devolve) new ways of seeing themselves. Such challenges do not succeed too often. Indeed the gap of sensibilities between artist and audience this century, with visual art so predominantly abstract, concert music harmonically dissonant, and literature linguistically experimental, has rendered communicativeness between artist and audience in a constant state of strain. In previous eras gaps between artist and audience certainly existed, but the general public seemed always to acknowledge, understand, and accept some innovations of previous generations. This has happened less frequently in recent decades. The type of artist who can thrive in this situation, as Arnold Schoenberg noted in praise of Charles Ives, is one who responds to neglect with contempt. Artists true to themselves but lacking in broader social anchoring can grow indulgent, however. Resenting isolation, such artists often engross their talents in attacks upon the world which fails to appreciate them. That which is shocking can then be pursued as an end itself, and the community of artists so inclined shuns colleagues who do not conform. Meanwhile much of the public comes to expect the shocking and blindly disregards it; a smaller, chic segment perversely enjoys it. Only a small minority discerns, understands, and finds genuine content and spiritual uplift. Such a deracinated state has been the norm throughout the twentieth century in free nations. The forced communicativeness in totalitarian states has provided no pathway out of the malaise. If anything, their example has further barred resolutions. Terms like "modern art" and "contemporary music" have come to have intellectually confronting rather than merely temporal connotations. When the government took on the role of funding some of the modern arts, this twentieth-century norm of a yawning gap of sensibility between artist and general society rendered clashes inevitable, for then the question of financial support magnifies all emotions.

Another backdrop in the hostility over the arts centers on the question of the arts' function in the public mind. After such incessant bombardment of confrontational art, the public appears to yearn for creative work of a more reinforcing nature. The desire for reinforcement itself has come to reveal pathological dimensions. Audiences are often utterly closed-minded, even narcissistic, in regard to their demands for reinforcement, and this alienation in the arts is but one dimension of a more generally depressed, lonely state of people in work, leisure, education, and romance. The self demands positive mirroring and resists ultimately with rage when challenged. In the arts, with public funding heightening a sense of entitlement, the outrage over perceived obscenity easily grows hysterical.

Conflicts between public self-entitlement and artists' *epaté le bourgeoisie* tendencies came to a head in 1989. The Endowment's administrative leadership and Presidentially nominated Council, all of whom were Reagan appointments, had approved, among their thousands of awards, the funding of several agencies which in turn granted support to individual artists. Two artists here drew fire, at first from Senator Jessie Helms of North Carolina. Others soon joined in a chorus of outrage, some with sincerity, others out of cynical political motives. The two artists in question were Andres Serrano and Robert Mapplethorpe. One of Serrano's work entitled "Piss Christ," featured a small crucifix submerged in a container of urine. Serrano may have been attempting to show his feelings about Christianity. He may have also sought to depict how he felt modern society treats the genuine Christian spirit (revealed by its attitude toward many artists). Knowing the outrage that would likely occur, he may have sought to reveal the irony of people preferring to view a man nailed to a cross over an inanimate statuette submerged in urine. Generally, the artistic intent was examined without much care. People were outraged; they responded narcissistically, a narcissism lent further entitlement by the fact of government largesse being involved. In such a state, the outrage could not easily be examined, but it could be readily exploited by skillful journalists and politicians. Outrage led to calls for wholesale examinations over whether the government ought be involved in such activities as the support of the arts.

The rage and the political crossfires around the publicly supported photographs of Robert Mapplethorpe were even more intense. In question was an exhibition of 150 of Mapplethorpe's photographs, first displayed in 1989 in Washington's Corcoran Gallery. Several photographs showed naked children. Ten, intentionally displayed on such an angle that one could not view them inadvertently, were homoerotic and racially intermixed in content. Mapplethorpe was a homosexual who had died of AIDS in the previous year. Phobias regarding AIDS, homosexuality, and race comprised a fearsome combination, something Mapplethorpe doubtlessly knew, though he did not compose the actual show. His supporters organized the display after his death. They saw Mapplethorpe as a great artist though few others had, and knew that the nature of his lifestyle and art would prove disturbing. But that, many contended, is one of the functions of art. Some rather crudely lambasted the exhibit. The Corcoran Gallery fearfully closed its show. In several other cities people tried to prevent the exhibit from appearing. The Cincinnati museum fought to present the photographs. Local prosecutors indicted the curator; he was ultimately acquitted.

The questions here involved definitions of art versus obscenity and demarcations as to community rights with respect to drawing bounds between obscenity and First Amendment rights. Outside the courts these questions tend not to concern the Federal government. But in the Arts and Humanities Endowments the government has to contend with the question of what standards or guidelines it sets with respect to eligibility even with respect to works deemed legitimate by court ruling or public consensus.

Back in 1938 Walker Evans' photographic series of the rural poor later featured in James Agee's *Let Us Now Praise Famous Men* went on display in New York. The works shocked many visitors to the exhibit because of the starkness with which the poverty, theretofore largely unseen, came forth. (And Evans had actually rearranged the interiors of sharecroppers homes to convey a sense of cleanliness and dignity.) Several unclothed young children were also photographed frontally. The shock in response to Evans' work focused on the photographs rather than on the fact that some government largesse had gone toward their preparation. With Robert Mapplethorpe's and Andres Serrano's work the chief accelerator to the outrage was the government support. Every day across the country vastly more obscene work is sold at magazine stands and in video stores. What was shocking about Mapplethorpe and Serrano certainly touched raw nerves regarding religion, homosexuality, AIDS, and racism, but there would have been hardly a ripple were no government funding at issue. (And neither artist would have ever gained much fame.) The Serrano and Mapplethorpe exhibits struck at the public's consciousness. Revealing the degree to which the public was primed, several months after the controversies broke the President of American University, under strange and sad psychological circumstances, was arrested for making obscene phone calls, and a joke around Washington had it that he was going to pay his phone bill with a grant from the National Endowment for the Arts.

People's sense of obscenity with respect to behavior or art seems to be held with a noblesse oblige attitude largely to private levels. With rising homicide rates, drug abuse, non-existent educational standards, and

crumbling families this traditional attitude has been undergoing fundamental challenges. The test of where a democratic society needs to draw
a line in regard to the banning any sort of behavior or creativity involves
the question of when people feel personally affected. The searing
impact of Mapplethorpe and Serrano stemmed from the sense of those
decaying values, which skillful politicians then cast as being exacerbated by government action. Politically right wing moralists argued that
the government should be actively countering the perceived decay in
American society. Jeffersonian traditions dictate that such moral flux
should resolve itself in private and community affairs, and that the
Federal government should play but a minimal role. Here then the perception that a Federal agency was actually magnifying a decaying moral
condition brought about objections from both conservative activists and
Jeffersonian libertarians.

The quantity spent on such "obscenity" per capita was amounted to
less than a day of Pentagon spending. Further the amount allocated to
such "moral" activities as military spending contributes infinitely more
to the national deficit, hence to inflation which has historically always
been the factor most responsible in a society's loosening values and
decadence, which the arts readily reflect. But such systematic concerns
have not informed the debates over government and the arts in the late
twentieth century. The public's posture of outrage over such obscenity
can indeed be cast as revealing a tendency typical in times of moral and
financial inflation: to seize upon a pseudo-issue, blow it out of proportion, and then collectively avoid, even deny more complicated and genuinely threatening questions. The polemics over the arts here involve a
conflict of narcissisms and their cynical exploitation by politicians and
journalists.

When the general problems of the human condition are so vast that
they boggle and intimidate even the astute observer, the malaise is easily manipulated by leaders who can give the impression that they have a
particular insight. Going back to the days of the Jacksonians' rhetoric
against John Quincy Adams, through some of the Populists, to Huey
Long, Joe McCarthy, and George Wallace, American politics has always
displayed a strain of cunning anti-intellectualism which, rather than
seeking to raise the vision of the citizenry, talks down to the lowest
common denominator. A sniggering jest which subsumes much of the
outwardly self-righteous indignation over Mapplethorpe and Serrano
was very much part of this tradition. It is an easy topic to masticate with
the folks back home, and it puts the sincere, systematic intellectual for-

ever on the defensive. Quantitatively the alleged waste is insignificant yet many hours are devoted to bashing here. Politically it works, but it further subverts the cultural unity which the Endowments are supposed to foster, and it overlooks deeper causes of the decay of values allegedly revealed here, causes rooted in the ruinous inflationary economic policies which many Endowment critics have endorsed.

The narrowness of many of the Endowment's critics has its counterpart among those at the opposite end of the issue. The narcissistic condition which skilled rhetoricians of the political right exploit is not exclusive to one political wing. Some of the defenders of the funding of a Mapplethorpe or a Serrano also employ *ad hominem* McCarthyist arguments of their own, asserting opponents oppose the First Amendment, lack appreciation of the arts, cling to outdated mores, and harbor racist and homophobic sensibilities. Just as the Helmsians charged certain artists with pursuing perversion for its own sake, both sides were (are) to some degree correct. Within each camp lie extremists. But the charges by the defenders of Mapplethorpe and Serrano reveal much of the same intolerance they have quickly criticized when leveled at themselves.

To contend with either extreme ultimately broaches Nietzschean questions—by what standard can one say that censorship is wrong? Why is free speech sacred? Such ultimately existential questions are worth asking if only as an intellectual exercise. They are similarly valuable in the context of the Humanities where of late they broach deconstructionist queries into the legitimacy of theretofore hierarchical axioms about ethical meaning and of any supposedly supportive philosophical and literary canons. But because Constitutional principles provide the basis for the government which provides the funding for work in the Humanities and the Arts, it would be incongruous of that body to pursue terribly much support of work oriented to the deconstruction of those very Constitutional principles. That same government would be, should be, loathe to intrude upon any such privately supported discourse. The dialectics of any such discourse are best left unintruded. The agency of government cannot be neutral. To remain uninvolved can constitute a form of support, given that subvention can prove co-optative.

The Humanities Endowment has thus largely refrained from involvement with deconstructionist modes of analysis which when applied to politics do ultimately question, and deconstruct, many principles of the Constitution. Meanwhile the law enforcement mechanisms of the same government ensure that private discourse over such questions occur without censorship or legal recrimination. With the same undergirding constitutional principles, but with much higher emotional stakes at hand, the Endowments have avoided much interaction with work which can be construed as obscene, while the Justice Department permits vastly more obscene expressions to take place every day in the private sector. The Endowments are clearly motivated in their judgments here by their recognition and anticipation of public pleasure or distaste with their judgments. This process is undeniably political and cannot be otherwise when public funding is involved. Audiences have as much right to petition a democratic government as do artists and scholars. In response, the government can impose admittedly slippery standards in regard to work to which it gives funding, while enforcing legal rights of expression in regard to much to which it refuses largesse. Great care has to be given in articulating standards here, and recognizing their changeability is essential. But standards can be imposed, and their imposition need not constitute censorship, though it can be dubbed so with great rhetorical flourish.

A chief complication in the debates here involves the problem of discipledom. Many humanists in various disciplines who embrace deconstructionist modes of inquiry, for example, simply execute them badly, in ways which grossly oversimplify or utterly contradict the ideas of such seminal thinkers in the genre as Michel Foucault, Mikhail Bakhtin, Paul de Man, and Jacques Derrida. Responses to criticism often involve hiding behind the great thinkers with a claim that critics do not understand or oppose for political reasons. Similarly, some critics of the modern art which attempts to shock for the sake of shocking are characterized as anti-art Yahoos. Some are. But the charges may as easily involve projection. At either end the disciples drag the discourse away from intelligent discourse or mediation. And it is on that ground that the public can and should expect, as well as even engage in, discussions over the allocations of its dollars. Certainly the middle ground can and often does exclude certain modes of discourse and expression, but such extremists have the logical option of refraining from engaging in the invariably corrupting processes of government.

The "taint" of government funding has raised several thorny issues about artistic purity. Several painters, notably Mark Rothko and Jackson Pollock, received W.P.A. assistance during the New Deal and subsequently felt ashamed of their "sellout." After 1945 they sought to demonstrate how minimally the flirtation with government had influenced their esthetic development. Indeed such a Romantic perspective exists among many artists and audiences that the best is pure, and purity is devoid of diverting political constraints. Yet an ambivalence grows when public funding is available. Denials or curtailments prompt defensive postures based on the "purity" ideals. Only those who neither seek nor accept public support are consistent here.

Accepting that some constraint is unavoidable, the criticism of government as *unduly* corrupting and intrusive compels a look at the impact of alternative modes of support. Here the major sources are the corporate sponsors. Historically they have tended to be even more esthetically conservative than the government. Theatre orchestras, opera houses, and ballets which rely on corporate funding, for example, have tended to emphasize the classics of their respective fields. Since 1965 Federal sponsorship has allowed greater exposure of contemporary works than would have otherwise occurred.

Public funds can be withheld from legal modes of expression. This is no contradiction. Trouble can emerge, however, if the procedures and guidelines prescribing what modes lie outside the bounds of eligibility for public support become too rigid and exclude work from which the collective public spirit could profit. But such questions go less to the issue of whether exclusions should be made and more to the matter of how and by whom. Members of the arts community generally confuse this distinction when they respond to the Mapplethorpe/Serrano controversies. They appeared to encase themselves, decried all critics as fascist homophobes, and declared all art was worthy of support. Other equally extremist views have been on hand in the public debate over arts funding, views which implied all modern art to be obscenity and nonsense and which opined that the NEA should be done away with altogether. This latter view appeared to have greater political impact. A few members of Congress went so far as to advocate shutting the Endowment down. Many more wanted the Endowment to give evidence of putting its house in such order as to prevent or ameliorate any future public brouhahas. To this end the Endowment leadership testified before Congress at times of reappropriation and discussed such questions of evaluation procedures and potential restrictions at the meeting of their own National Council. In reaction to the very existence of such discussions, irrespective of their content, groups and individuals reacted reflexively. Reducing all such criticism as homophobic responses to the Mapplethorpe photographs, one group interrupted a meeting of the Arts Council in May, 1990 chanting "We're queer, and we're here!" Behaving much like the National Rifle Association, such groups prefer not to join in the political processes to find legitimate solutions to issues involving public safety and ethics. Instead these interested parties have dug in their heels and rhetorically cast all who seek any revisions in the status quo beyond increased latitude and entitlement as part of the forces bent on destroying the first and second amendments to the Constitution. The media has played up this extremism with the sad logic that the public gives more attention to such spectacles than to the proceedings of sober gatherings.

Amidst these crossfires, in 1990 the Chairman of the National Endowment for the Arts, John Frohnmeyer, floated the idea of grant recipients signing an oath, promising to refrain from activities and expressions when using the grant that could be construed as obscene. This led to further furor concerning censorship. It also prompted legal challenges. The challenges were successful, for the Federal courts decided that such a concern as obscenity required a legal definition which only a court could render. Once broached the question of obscenity in the context of public spending seems to self compound, and attempts to put the matter to rest merely jangle more nerves among the interested parties. The Endowment continues to grapple here with the concept of "decency." As long as the issue appears an easy topic with which certain politicians can call attention to themselves, other needless aggravations will regularly enter the arena as well.

Should such nerve wracking political problems continue, the Endowment's leadership and Congressional supporters may have to consider such a risky maneuver as asking the President to invite onto the National Council several major figures whose credentials are unimpeachable in the minds of the Endowments' most extreme opponents. Since the first term of Ronald Reagan, the Arts and Humanities Councils were filled with Republicans, but the perception remained among the extreme (let-Reagan-be-Reagan) right that the Arts Endowment has not received sufficient policing. This Republican wing was been suspicious of even the moderate Republicans in many contexts, and from their ranks calls for the outright abolition of the Arts Endowment grew. With tight budgets, such views maintained a presence, even though the elimination of the Endowments would make little impact with respect to the national debt or to such enormous crises as the Savings and Loan and HUD debacles of the late 1980s and early 90s. But any controversies like the Mapplethorpe exhibit make opposition to the Endowment politically irresistible. Bringing the extreme opposition "on board" mollifies the far right.

Back in the 1930s when Hallie Flanagan ran the WPA Theatre Project, her undeniable credentials in the field, combined with her inexhaustible administrative attention to all details around her, generally kept many Congressional critics at bay. With a more diffuse Arts Endowment, such expertise at the helm is impossible to conceive, as no one could command all the arts as Flanagan did the theatre. Further John Frohnmeyer, NEA Chairman under George Bush, was not an artist. Though sympathetic to the arts in many ways, Frohnmayer was an attorney. More an indication than a cause of the state of affairs between government and the arts, the appointment of a lawyer to run the bureaucracy reveals, perhaps, how the government and the arts have paradoxically grown apart since being united in 1965. A practicing artist, with an actual record of art to be scrutinized would likely be too great a risk as an appointment. Like Henry Alsberg of the Federal Writers' Project, many such artists prove inept with the complex banalities of bureaucracy anyway. But a non professional artist, while more than capable as an administrator can perhaps please neither the artistic community nor many Congressional overseers, particularly in an age of esthetic and philosophical polarization.

In the wake of the blasts against the NEA by Jessie Helms and others, Frohnmayer attempted an ill-fated counter offensive by defending the rights of artists and the sanctity of free speech and expression. While his defense was noble, there was nothing new in it (how could there be?). Furthermore, Frohnmayer did not have the access to the media and the notability of his agency's Congressional critics. Compared to a distemperate verbal blast at apparently government-supported homosexuality, a small government agency director's undramatic defense of First Amendment rights was not good press copy. The broadsides from Helms and others amounted to attacks on the arts communities and on the Bush Administration. Frohnmayer's counterpoint appeared a most weak response, for his defense was to be fully expected, and, pivotally, no one higher in the Bush Administration made any similar statements of support. Frohnmayer appeared to have been left on his own by the White House. He further isolated himself more than he needed to, for he defended not his agency but the rights of artists. In hindsight he should have realized that artists are more than capable of defending themselves. He was not their spokesperson. Had he defended the NEA—the sobriety of its screening processes, its contributions to the American public, the efficiency of its operation (only ten per cent of its budget spent on internal administration), and the meager size of its budget overall—he would have followed Socrates' dictum of "doing his job" and not another's. And such a well-honed defense of just the agency would not have as easily isolated himself from the White House. Instead the Bush Administration's silence left him dangling. Even the leadership of the neighboring NEH was disassociatively silent. The Bush Administration then used Frohnmayer and the NEA in a bigger game of Presidential politics. In the early months of the 1992 Presidential Primaries, right wing Republican challenger Pat Buchanan ran reasonably well in New Hampshire and Georgia. Some of Buchanan's campaign commercials criticized Bush via a pillorying of the NEA. In response to the glimmers of strength that Buchanan showed in those two states, Bush "accepted John Frohnmayer's resignation." Frohnmayer subsequently wrote a book in which he appeared largely to whine about how such a well-intentioned gentleman as he was savaged by cruel politics. Like the pure artist, the only logical position such a pure soul can take is one of non-involvement.

Frohnmayer's successor, Anne Imelda Redice tried to put a more conservative fight-the-nonsense face on her leadership, but the agency itself continued to bear scrutiny from political groups who oppose it, no matter its processes, because it has become a convenient symbol of a government purportedly no longer of, by, or for the people. When William Clinton took office in 1993 he took five months to nominate historian Sheldon Hackney to head the NEH and seven months to name actress Jane Alexander to head the NEA. The wounds of the Serrano and Mapplethorpe controversies lingered. In 1992 Representative Philip Crane of Illinois moved to end the NEA. The House voted against the proposal 329-85. In 1993 the same bill came forth. The Endowment again survived, but the opposition had grown, with the vote being 322-105. The House reduced the NEA budget from $174.9 million to $166.2; the Senate restored the cut.[16] Cuts have continued ever since. The 1994 Republican "Contract with America" called for the total elimination of the Arts and Humanities Endowments.

Beyond the many pitfalls and political crossfires that rage over matters of obscenity and deconstruction, and over the NEA's and NEH's legitimacy, the arts and humanities endowments must also wrestle with the definitions and categories of their funded endeavors. On the surface this would appear to be a mere matter of classification, but it is more complex, and the complexity has permitted some politically risky work to receive funds. There are, of course, the traditional classifications in the arts and humanities—music, art, drama; history, philosophy, literature. But in the arts especially certain categories have emerged which, in part, seem to be new and innovative, while to others they appear as masks for activities inappropriate for government funding or, to some, inappropriate for the arts altogether. "Performance art" is a most controversial example here which has further engendered journalistic and Congressional controversy.

In 1990 Karen Finlay indirectly received government support for "performance art." Her performance involved, among other things, her dancing freely on stage after smearing her nude body with chocolate and bean sprouts. The bean sprouts symbolized sperm; the chocolate implied the defiling of women during love making. The controversies surrounding this grant went back to the same obscenity issues that arose with respect to Mapplethorpe and Serrano. Few questioned whether Finlay had the right to express herself as she did. Legal censorship was never broached in any locale where she performed. Some did raise the question of whether her work constitutes art. In itself that could and cannot be resolved to the satisfaction of interested parties. The similarity of her activity to some traditional striptease dancing revealed a paradox within many feminist groups which favor Finlay but continue to seek censorship of striptease as pornography. Such contradictions go ignored. Traditional right-wing groups consistently oppose both. Old fashioned hyper-masculine contradictions which would likely favor striptease but oppose Finlay were not explicitly present in the discourse over the topic, though there the distinction could be raised that strip joints do not receive tax support. The argument favoring the freedom of expression for either type of dancing rests in part on each constituting art. Courts continue to wrestle with the issue, and resolutions vary with judges, with attorneys, with the bludgeoning interested parties experience from politically interested groups, and with the heart-felt mandates of public opinion.

As with Mapplethorpe, in the Finlay case a question independent of her work's legality involved whether she should receive public funds. This question further illustrates the different and often contrasting functions of government. The Endowments can deem certain works inappropriate with respect to their domain, while the Courts' simultaneously judge them to be legitimate.

The Finlay case also brought forth the issue of the acceptability of entire classifications or genres. One major development in the arts since the establishment of the Endowments has involved a proliferation of new, often self-conscious categories. While no "conspiracy" lay beneath here, styles of art have more easily gained acceptance within agencies as categories than as individual works within older categorical settings. Criticism and rejection within traditional genres is readily written off as a matter of taste, but criticism of a category can be more easily labeled prejudice. This allows judgments to become esthetically banal and politically narrow. At the point of the acceptance of a genre within a bureaucracy, the potential political objections are immediate while serious esthetic questions are not at hand, as no individual examples are necessarily atop the agenda. So acquiescence readily occurs. Once established, the categories seek esthetic criteria while feuds over criticism maintain a desultory and narrow political vocabulary. The problem is the criteria are limited, as is the quantity of accepted practitioners within the genre. This reveals itself during many Endowment evaluation proceedings. Peer review panels are pivotal in this regard. Compared with established genres the newness of the category limits the size of the pool of potential reviewers. The self consciousness and often the defensiveness among the activists in the genre can also limit the careful probing expected in a peer review. One member of the National Arts Council, literary historian and critic Joseph Epstein of Northwestern University, commented here:

> If the field is weak the grants are going to be shaky, because the peers are from those fields, and they are giving grants to people like themselves. ... In those fields where there are no real standards, except a vague feeling that "Gee, it works," or "it clicks," there is nothing very concrete going on. When you read the panel evaluations on these grants, you feel they are intellectually very thin.[17]

Problems of back-scratching, even if inadvertent, appear more difficult to avoid in new genres. The self-conscious, in-the-bunker mentality of many sympathizers hides blemishes and accentuates suspicions in regard to any criticism, no matter how well meaning. And some of the self-consciousness of genre generates a keener pursuit of the shocking as an end in itself. Criticism is dismissed with a McCarthyist vocabulary.

With such battles it can be bureaucratically easier simply to declare all performance art, or any other such category, ineligible. That risks cutting off potential support from excellent and deserving work which could well serve the public spirit with but a modicum of aid. As bureaucracies mature they have a tendency to harden in ways which avoid internal procedural difficulties. Thus in one political climate a genre can be added. In another it can be dumped. The art within can recede in the debates at either end as a bureaucracy's concern with survival eclipses its mission to serve those to whom its original legislative mandate directed it. If genres are cut, the deserving clients frozen out become the visible victims in the media, just as the earlier controversial items had been visible before. Then the entire bureaucracy is suspect by its general restrictiveness rather than by its specific errors. The dissonance in such public perceptions about obscenity will not likely fade away from the national political discourse. As performance art becomes linked to it, the genre can fall from the status of official recognition. Emphases on gifts in matching have tended to favor the mainstream which gains most from private sources. With such controversies as those over performance art, the tendency toward the mainstream will likely grow. And conservative organizations like the Heritage Foundation have voiced such concerns here, declaring that the Endowments are not giving sufficient support to mainstream traditions.

At the heart of the discussions over mainstream versus fringe art lies the philosophical and public policy questions of what ought be the relationship between government and the society's margins. Focusing on the mainstream invites charges that the government is standing in the way of the natural exchange that occurs between innovators and conservatives. But the counterargument has it that all innovation is not necessarily valid, that such fringes are best left unco-opted, and that many who claim to be part of the avant garde often merely use the label as an honorific while hardly belonging in the class of the true innovators of the past. (Many even on the left would admit, for example, that Mapplethorpe became "great" only after the NEA controversy.) Debate will continue, as will distrust and name calling on either side.

Another "classification" issue involves the racial, ethnic, religious and gender bases of works. The Endowments do not discriminate against any such groups in their internal administration or in their granting decisions. There have never been any successful suits against either agency along any such lines. Indeed the Endowments have gone to considerable lengths to expose and elevate the histories and arts of these groups. Historically black institutions, for example, receive special preferences with respect to institutional grants. Certain tensions emerge over the question of such classifications, tensions both intellectual and political in nature. The elevation of women's music, for example, serves well to help debunk the silly old myth that "there has never been a great female composer." The tension exists here in the art itself being potentially incidental to the celebration of the gender (or race or ethnicity) at hand. The art that may lie independent of the race or gender can easily be ignored or distorted. Many artists eschew such identity and see themselves, for example, as "painters who happened to be Jewish" rather than as "Jewish painters." When the great music teacher Nadia Boulanger conducted the Boston Symphony Orchestra in 1937, the first woman ever to do so, she was asked by an energetic reporter how it felt to be the first woman to conduct a great orchestra. Condescendingly, she replied: "Monsieur, I have been a woman for over fifty years now, and I have gotten over my original astonishment." Similarly, the composer R. Nathaniel Dett sought no identity as a black man and preferred to seek dignity as an artist independent of the happenstance of his race. Thus while celebrations of women's art, African-American theatre, or Jewish music can portray racial, gender, or ethnically defined content, they can also overlook and oversimplify other esthetic content which may be as salient, if not more so. There is no one correct approach here, but the late twentieth-century emphasis on "cultural diversity" in education, the arts, and humanities research risks one dimensionality. This risk is heightened by the "diversity" defenders' tendency to respond to most criticism with reflexive charges of racism, sexism, and ethnocentricity. The result is a potential encasing of the varieties of creative activities into a series of discreet and overly narrow categories. Paradoxically this denies much diversity within each designated group.

The potential lack of actual diversity within the orthodoxy of "diversity" creates further risks in the context of public funding of pertinent activities. For in the reviewing procedures at the Endowments, the racial, gender, and ethnic labels have each come to earn the status of criterion. Here, independent of the issue of discrimination, the Endowments risk inadvertently supporting the "Black artist" over the "artist who happens to be black." This trap of essentialism plagues much discourse over general academic fields like Women's Studies, African American Studies, and scholarship on ethnicity. The intellectual questions here take on political content when Endowment funds are at stake, as well as when the desires for the visibility of certain groups engenders greater pressure for results often measured with but bare statistics. Risks grow of a loosening of intellectual standards in the evaluation of competing applications. This yields rhetorical possibilities to critics, hostile to such concerns regarding race, gender, ethnicity, or general diversity having any influence on the criteria by which funds are allocated for the arts and humanities. Such crossfires are unavoidable as the Endowments seek both a fostering of the arts and humanities in their best abstract forms as well as with respect to many identifying features which may tinge some of their character. The problem that appears to be growing here stems from the fact that much art requires viewers to accept the vision of another, even if the vision clashes with their own. When viewers grow sufficiently narcissistic to render such trusting acceptance impossible a vital process in art is lost, and such narcissists will then turn to angrily at a government, or any agency, which supports anything that fails to give them personal reinforcement and gratification to which they feel entitled.

Such crosscurrents flow in the marketplaces of arts and ideas. The problem for government agencies concerned with such matters is that these conflicts cannot be left on a strictly implicit basis. If many people storm out of a theatre, management takes note. As with "obscenity" controversies, the Endowments' leaders must respond to public outcries and navigate a treacherous course. Need they ultimately consider sacrificing a few, even well-deserving initiators, sacrificing "excellence" for "diversity" or vice versa, to show they stand firmly against points which raise the hackles of some Congressmen potentially able to pull the financial plug on their entire operation? Critics of such questions would assert rhetorically that excellence and diversity are not opposites, and indeed they are not. But they are not always identical, and where they are not finances require choices be made, choices which quickly grow politicized.

The Humanities Endowment has had fewer such public and Congressional concerns than has the Arts Endowment. The Humanities many programs have appeared generally acceptable, that which is ruled unacceptable has not struck many raw nerves among Congressmen or the public at large. But there are heated issues, particularly those which involve education. A frustration of the Humanities Endowment appears to lie in the minimal degree to which it can shape the educational agenda of the nation. Aside from Bully Pulpit rhetoric against the perceived decaying standards of American education, the NEH can apply little direct pressure. Hosting and funding various conferences, lectures, and programs on this topic generally state and restate known points of view and risk preaching to the choir. As long as the educational institutions of the country continue to flounder and the power over them rests largely at state and local levels, this Federal frustration will likely continue. Yet concerns for educational quality continue to be raised and the Endowment is often caught in crossfires.

In the National Endowment for the Arts the stakes appear higher because of public sensitivity. Artists like Finley and Mapplethorpe, and, even more, their supporters, regularly claim their opponents harbor prejudices which deserve no countenance. At the same time many such supporters claim their preferences are part, even the essence, of their esthetic outlook and deserving of support as a legitimate genre. Here then the potential middle ground which ignores the life styles of artists and focuses strictly on the art is rejected as part of the opposition. The message thus cannot be separated from the messenger. Meanwhile, the public and Congressional opposition to the content of such art as well as to the lifestyles of such artists must be contended. Oaths promising no commerce with obscenity are tossed out in the courts. Defining "decency" becomes a complete morass. The Endowment may ultimately have to make the calculation that the noisy anti-homophobic groups and other supporters simply cannot be indulged, no matter how the media focuses on them. Charges of censorship will arise from within the Arts Council as well as from the public, the press and Congress, and they will have to be weathered. The Endowment will come to be seen as a "mainstream" institution which insufficiently supports the fringes of the arts community that have allegedly shaped so many new directions. In time, likely, other fringes will largely forget that fight and successfully petition the Endowment for other support, causing other controversies to arise. These battles will perhaps form a more creative dialectic for government and the arts than would one of greater indulgence of current fringes. For Congress could seriously cut or even abolish the Endowment if such indulgence were seen to continue. The result would be a domination of funding by private groups which would be yet more "mainstreaming" in its impact. Additionally many of those fringes have within themselves become rather conservative intolerant orthodoxies when in positions of petty power.

Another response to political pressures surrounding "obscenity" has involved greater portions of budget allocations to individual states. In 1990 the Endowment's "national" allocation rose by but $3 million while money to be turned over to state Endowment's rose $12 million, $6 million in unrestricted block grants, $6 million which the NEA would oversee. The results were roughly 500 fewer national grants, smaller allocations among the surviving ones, and cuts of roughly fifteen percent in individual Endowment Programs. The state/Federal administrative structure risks simply adds additional layers of bureaucracy to the process of allocation. Greater power given to individual states, superfi-

cially more democratic and supportive of "diversity," increases susceptibility to anti-intellectual, populist pressures. Further, money with which
states themselves support their Arts Endowments, will easily be trimmed
from budgets with some Federal dollars flowing in. The result is fewer
public funds going to the arts.

The questions of "diversity" and the structure of Federalism continually weaken America's efforts at supporting the arts. Consideration of
the question of public of support of the arts in, for example, Germany
can commence with certain assumptions. One would not have to ask a
German whether or not Beethoven was a significant figure in German
history. The same would hold with respect to Shakespeare in England,
Cezanne in France, Verdi in Italy, or Tolstoy in Russia. Indeed natives
of those countries would likely scoff in stupefication at the introduction
of such a thought and may even inquire as to the questioners intelligence
or sanity. Yet in the United States there lies a strong strain within the
political fabric which deems it fitting to discourse over whether there is
sufficient historical significance in Edgar Allan Poe, Mary Cassatt,
Eugene O'Neill, Louis Sullivan, Langston Hughes or Charles Ives to
justify significant outlays of public funds. Judgments as to whether such
questions ought to be asked yield but bare opinions. The fact is that the
nature of American culture is such that these questions are seriously
raised, to the degree that the anti-intellectualism within has itself
become a political tradition. Several factors have set the bases here, and
others, more contemporary, have magnified it.

Anti-elite, utilitarian,* and populist sentiments have always held traditionally defined "culture" with suspicion, so most any official culture
was suspect as well. The diversity of the American population has also

---

*In *Contested Truths*, Daniel Rodgers endeavors to challenge the wide-
ly-held perspective that nineteenth-century America was a strongly utilitarian culture on the basis that the nation had no tradition of utilitarianism a la Jeremy Bentham in Great Britain. But his argument misses a
key point—that a formalized, written tradition on the subject achieving
such systematization as to earn an "ism" suffix itself reveals a lesser
degree of utilitarianism. An intellectual tradition of utilitarianism risks
self contradiction. Bentham's writings reveal that British society was not
what he wished it to be. What is deemed a "puzzling failure" of a
Bentham in America is not so much puzzling as it is further revealing of
the strength of the tradition Bentham promoted. This is what Tocqueville
meant when he described America as the society in which the ideas of
Descartes are read least and practiced most.[18]

ignited fears of any one culture overly burdening others. In the late twentieth century when certain officially designated minorities have been able to make political gains by highlighting differences between themselves and other groups, this fear has every political reason to grow. Indeed "diversity" in this late twentieth-century form has become a virtual leitmotif in any discourse over arts and educational issues, often to the destruction of the spiritual uplift the arts and humanities can engender and upon which their official support has been predicated. As a catch-all, "diversity" has risked replacing the deeper spiritual value of a given work, object, or theme with a more pedestrian narrative label identifying the creator. Such labels can augment the spiritual dimension but can be peripheral or even have a negative impact by the promotion of narcissism. While Germans do not even consider whether Beethoven is significant with respect to their culture, many Americans have come to consider virtually nothing but such questions. Here labels regarding ethnicity, race, region, gender, etc. enter and risk providing not so much an answer but an illusory replacement to content. The useful and stimulating discourse over the question of what makes an item significant to a culture thus freezes. Intelligent questions are not addressed but merely displaced by concern over political patronage. The new discourse over culture simply amounts to conflicts between competing political constituencies. Questions of the role and value of culture and the proper manners of promotion are largely ignored. When public funds are on hand, popular impatience over the childish and incestuous nature of such discourse among alleged experts is inevitable.

American traditions of anti-intellectualism and "diversityistic" nomenclature have invaded the worlds of the arts and humanities to subvert much of the very cultural work designed to negate devolution into such pedestrianism in the first place. This state of affairs has been exacerbated by the abstract, elusive nature of many major currents in the modern arts and humanities. Gertrude Stein once commented that "everything destroys itself in the twentieth century and nothing continues." Such intellectual and artistic fashions which seem ephemeral and impenetrable, as well as occasionally shocking and obscure, place government agencies intent on promoting the arts and humanities for the public good in a precarious position. The artists and other potential recipients themselves face challenges here as well. For both they and the agencies may tend to avoid controversy by gravitating toward older, safer mainstream esthetics, leaving various "cutting edges" alone. This can accentuate the secessionism of those left on the margins and leave the "center" guided by political concerns as much as esthetic ones. This happened in the 1930s when the writers found the work of the WPA Writers' Project basically artless. The era's important innovations in literature went forward independent of, and in some ways in spite of, the government's work. This situation prompted poet W.H. Auden to opine that such government efforts are noble yet absurd. A government agency needs to group recipients into a class, while, Auden noted, every artist constitutes a class of one. Though Auden's characterization is extreme, it encapsulates the ultimate dilemma in which any government body and creative person find him or herself when attempting some sort of commerce. The government demands some form of guideline and compliance; the artist desires freedom. The two need not always but ultimately must conflict. Given the controversies with some solitary moderns like Finlay, Serrano, and Mapplethorpe, and the success of collective efforts in the thirties, group projects may gain greater favor, as will art forms and styles which are more devoted to communication than just to expression. This will be problematic for such approaches were very much of the times in the thirties. In the late twentieth century they appear old fashioned and out of step. The depressing, alienated tone of much modern art has also less of a rhetorical base in a post-Cold War world. Now the Russians allow modern art, so America's support for art in the context of a broader ideological battle for world sympathy is no longer relevant. Without the Cold War motive, the charges of decadence loom without any counterweight. And with growing fears of AIDS, homosexuality, and sacrilegiousness in a budget-conscious political arena, the atmosphere is fearsome. Research in science, which also undergoes criticism, has an aura of linearity and progress to justify itself before funding agencies. The arts can present no such progressive aura.

The depressing tone of some modern art and of intellectual life more generally makes support a very tough sell. In parallel, commenting on the nature of intellectual life in Vienna at the turn of the century in the age of Freud, psychiatrist Bruno Bettelheim was struck by the fact that the efflorescence of the Viennese intelligentsia coincided with the relative decline of Austria-Hungary as a significant power in the economic, political, and military affairs of Europe. Bettelheim saw this as a key backdrop in the development of such thinking as that of his master, Sigmund Freud, as well as more generally in the internally self-focused drama, art, and philosophy of pre-World War I Vienna. His perspective has pertinence to the life of so many Western artists and intellectuals in the twentieth century where, as Gertrude Stein said, "everything self-destructs and nothing continues," where the lessons of the arts and humanities are cast as not mere irrelevant but sometimes dangerous, where students at Stanford University can march and chant in self-clubbed unison: "Hey hey, ho ho, Western Culture's got to go." In similar circumstances Bettelheim's beloved Viennese found repose in the notion of life being "desperate but not serious." Such a rest is less tenable in a world in which nuclear destruction, environmental disaster, and terrorism threaten all. The notion that life can go on no matter the political and military burdens had the appearance of legitimacy before World War I. Since then such a pose has seemed more purely escapist and genteel than creative and noble. The more compelling state of military, environmental and political affairs ultimately intrudes onto the arts and humanities, especially when they are receiving public support.[19]

The call for accountability has more than arbitrary guidelines. In Freud's Vienna the shocking and superficially irrelevant could be indulged with the sense that their ultimate worth could prove very different than contemporary judgments. What Bettelheim described as the inward turn of the Viennese "opened vast vistas unfettered by the public concerns of the day." With public expenditures, the supporting of such explicitly introspective work arouses criticism. The content may be shocking. The shocked have the right to petition their protests, and the supported have to respond to their ultimate benefactors. The undeniably legitimate problems of the human condition, to the amelioration of which all the work of the government can be considered ultimately devoted, can create an implicit litmus test of worthiness—does the work help or hurt? Usually those who ask such questions already have an answer in mind. Kantian arguments to the contrary are not heeded or even understood. The exchange between the political and creative worlds is thus limited. This has not occurred as a result of government activism in culture but because vastly larger forces have overtaken both the political and creative worlds. A popularly elected government cannot but reflect this.

Back in 1844 when Alexandre Vattemare petitioned the Congress for its approval of an exchange system between the major libraries of the major Western nations, Daniel Webster wrote in praise of the initiative. In a note of support he intoned the cry of Ajax from Homer's Iliad—"that my own eyes may behold." He scribbled the quotation in the original Greek. While few legislators of Webster's day possessed his degree of erudition in the Classics, none have anything close to it today. Schooling in ancient languages may not provide leaders with direct means to solve the colossal troubles that face them. But the contrast with Webster underscores the point that a vastly diminished core of learning now exists upon which all can agree to be a basis for the society's thought and action. Indeed some leaders regularly accumulate political capital by railing against any such notions of a cultural core. Amidst such a morass of spoils seeking, many in the public appear to yearn for some form of renewal.

Whether public agencies can foster such a renewal is debatable. For the procedures and labyrinths inherent in any such agency can best serve those who work best in such an undeniably politicized context. Those who spew against notions of a core culture, even with simple minded one-dimensionality, actually fit such a context very well. The thoughtful, clear-headed soul, who can envision a complex culture to be nurtured and promoted, must indeed recognize and take in many perspectives, including the uni-dimensionals. And if leaders, with little of the Classical patience for carefully drawn, moderately toned, complex thoughts readily respond to the loud and simplistic, the scenario of "the best lacking all conviction while the worst are full of passionate intensity" will prove ever more valid.

Shortly before his death in 1970, historian Richard Hofstadter consciously parodied his famous *Age of Reform* when he referred to the era of the late 1960s as an "age of rubbish." His sense was that many of the self-absorbed movers and shakers of modern politics were more frivolous clowns than serious radicals. In the generation since Hofstadter's death the legacy of the superficially heady days of the late 60s has indeed piled up much rubbish which attempts to pass for serious art, thought, education, and culture. And a warmed-over egalitarianism has demanded that the well-springs of many such activities be given opportunities at access to public resources allocated for the arts and humanities. Institutions have yielded to political pressures. The vast majority of work in the arts and humanities, publicly funded and otherwise, remains serious, substantial, and politically non-controversial. But the silly fringes continue to risk torpedoing the broader endeavors. It is many of these silly fringes that seem to engross the lion's share of public, press, Congressional, and internal staff concerns within and around the government sponsorship work in the arts. To the degree to which this is a growing cancer, it signifies a broader illness in the society which the arts, humanities, educational institutions, and the government can only reflect. This could then reveal T.S. Eliot's prophecy that civilization might not end on a bang but a whimper. If Hofstadter is correct, as he usually was, and thc issue is more one of trash than cancer, then with or without government subvention we'll simply best muddle through it.

Notes

1. Henry James, *Portrait of a Lady* (London: Penguin Editions, 1970), pp. viii-ix.

2. Paul Conkin, *The New Deal*, p. 101.

3. Ezra Pound, *Antheil and the Treatise on Harmony* (Chicago: Pascal Covici Publishers, 1927), p. 61.

4. John Dewey, *Art as Experience* (New York: Mouton, Balch and Co., 1934), p. 344.

5. Robert Hutchins, *The Higher Learning in America* (Chicago: University of Chicago Press, 1936, p. 95.}

6. John Dewey, *Freedom and Culture* (New York: Putnams', 1939), p. 49.

7. see Dewey, "Anti-Naturalism in Extremis," *The Partisan Review*, 1943.

8. *New York Times Magazine*, October 26, 1952, p. 32.

9. quoted in *The Report of the Commission on the Humanities* (New York, 1964), V, pp. 2-5 and in the National Foundation on the Arts and the Humanities Act, Public Law 89-209, (Washington, 1965), pp. 1-2.

10. see Joseph Horowitz, *The Ivory Trade, Music and the Business of Music at the Van Cliburn International Piano Competition* (New York: Summit Books, 1990), pp. 21-31.

11. Murrow to Senator Clairborne Pell, September 11, 1962, *Hearings Before a Special Subcommittee of the United States Senate Committee on Labor and Public Welfare,* S. 741, S. 785, and S. 1250, 87th Congress, 2d Session, (Washington, 1962), pp. 54-71; see also Morton Sosna, "The NEH and Cultural Nationalism," presentation to the Organization of American Historians, Washington, March 22, 1990.

12. Testimony before the U.S. House of Representatives, Economic Conditions of the Performing Arts; *Hearings before the Select Subcommittee on Education of the Committee on Education and Labor*, 87th Congress, 1st and 2d Sessions, 1961-62, p. 426.

13. *Hearings Before the Special Subcommittee on the Arts of the Committee on Labor and Public Welfare, United States Senate on S. 165 and S. 1316*, 88th Congress, 1st Session, (Washington, 1963), pp. 50-54.

14. *Congressional Record*, 89th Congress, 1st Session (Washington, 1965), p. 23937; *Senate Joint Hearings*, 1965, p. 7.

15. see, for example, Paul Conkin, *The New Deal*, (Arlington Heights, Ill.: AHM Publishing Corporation, 1975).

16. *Washington Post*, July 16, 1993, Section C, pp. 1-2.

17. *New York Times*, August 14, 1990, pp. 13-14.

18. Daniel T. Rodgers, *Contested Truths: Key Words in American Politics Since Independence*, (New York: Basic Books, 1987), pp. 17-24.

19. Bruno Bettelheim, *Freud's Vienna and Other Essays*. (New York: Vintage Press, [1956] 1991), p. 7.

Bibliography

In addition to the records of the House and Senate in the National Archives and the files of the office of the Architect of the Capitol in Washington, the following comprise the published sources consulted in preparation of this manuscript.

Aaron, Daniel, *Writers on the Left: Episodes in American Literary Communism.* New York, 1961.

Alsberg, Henry G. ed., *The American Guide.* New York, 1949.

American Philosophical Society, *Early Proceedings: Old Minutes of the Society form 1743-1838.* Philadelphia, 1884.

Andrews, Wayne, *Architecture, Ambition and Americans, A Social History of American Architecture.* New York, 1947.

Arian, Edward, *The Unfulfilled Promise: Public Subsidy of the Arts in America.* Philadelphia, 1989.

Berman, Elanor D., *Jefferson Among the Artists.* New York, 1947.

Boorstin, Daniel J. *America and the Image of Europe.* New York, 1960.

_____, *The Americans: The Colonial Experience.* New York, 1958.

_____, The Americans: The National Experience. New York, 1963.

Brooks, Van Wyck, *The Flowering of New England.* New York, 1936.

_____, *America Coming of Age.* New York, 1916.

Carpenter, Paul, *Music: An Art and a Business.* Norman, Okla., 1950.

Charles, Searle F., *Minister of Relief: Harry Hopkins and the Great Depression.* Syracuse, 1963.

Charvat, William, *The Origins of American Critical Thought, 1810-35.* Philadelphia, 1936.

Clark, Eliot H., *The History of the National Academy of Design, 1825-1953.* New York, 1954.

Conkin, Paul, *The New Deal,* rev. ed. Arlington Heights, Ill., 1975.
Cowdrey, Many Bartlett, ed., *The American Academy of Fine Arts and the American Art-Union.* 2 vols., New York, 1953.
Cripe, Helen. *Thomas Jefferson and Music.* Charlottesville, 1974.
Cummings, M.C. and Katz, R., *The Patron State.* New York, 1987.
Curti, Merle, *The Growth of American Thought.* New York, 1943.
Dargent, J.L., *Alexandre Vattemare.* Brussles, 1976.
Dies, Martin, *Martin Dies' Story.* New York, 1963.
DiMaggio, Paul J., *Nonprofessional Entertainment in the Arts: Studies in Mission and Constraint.* New York, 1986.
Dorian, Frederick, *Commitment to Culture: Art Patronage in Europe, Its Significance for America.* Pittsburgh, 1961.
Dow, G.P., *The Arts and Crafts in New England.* Topsfield, Ma., 1927.
Dunlap, William, *History of American Theatre.* New York, 1832.
DuPree, A. Hunter, *Science in the Federal Government, A History of Policies and Activities to 1940.* Cambridge, 1957.
Fairman, Charles E., *Art and Artists of the Capitol.* Washington, 1927.
Field, A., M. O'Hare., and J.M.D. Schuster, *Patrons Despite Themselves: Taxpayers and Arts Policy.* New York, 1983.
Flanagan, Hallie, *Arena.* New York, 1940.
Flexner, James T., *First Flowers of the American Wilderness. An Examination of Art and Society in Colonial America.* Boston, 1947.
_____, *That Wilder Image; The Painting of America's Native School from Thomas Cole to Winslow Homer.* Boston, 1962.
Gilbert, James B., *Writers and Partisans.* New York, 1968.
Goodman, Walter, The Committee: *The Extraordinary Career of the House Committee on Un-American Activities.* New York, 1968.
Greyser, Stephen A., ed., *Cultural Policy and Arts Administration.* Cambridge, Mass., 1973.
Hall, James and Barry Ubanov, *Modern Culture and the Arts.* New York, 1972.
Hall, Peter D., *The Organization of American Culture, 1700-1900: Private Institutions, Elites, and the Origins of American Nationality.* New York, 1984.
Handlin, Oscar, *This Was America.* Cambridge, 1949.
Harris, Niel, *The Artist In American Society.* New York, 1966.
Hazelton, George C., *The National Capitol, Its Architecture and History.* New York, 1908.
Hellman, Geoffrey T. *The Smithsonian Octopus on the Mall.* Philadelphia, 1967.

Hofstadter, Richard, *Anti-Intellectualism in American Life*. New York, 1963.

Howard, Donald, *The WPA and Federal Relief Policy*. New York, 1943.

Isham, Samuel, *A History of American Painting*. New York, 1927.

Jeffri, Joan, *Arts and Money*. New York, 1983.

Jensen, Merrill, *The New Nation*. New York, 1950.

Jones, Howard Mumford, *O Strange World, American Culture: The Formative Years*. New York, 1964.

Josephson, Matthew, *Infidel in the Temple*. New York, 1967.

Kazin, Alfred, *On Native Grounds: An Interpretation of Modern American Prose Literature*. New York, 1942.

Kohn, Hans, *American Nationalism*. New York, 1957.

Kouwenhoven, John A. *Made in America*. Garden City, 1962.

Larkin, Oliver W., *Art and Life in America*. New York, 1960.

———, *Samuel F.B. Morse and American Democratic Art*. Boston, 1954.

Larson, Gary O., *The Reluctant Patron: The United States Government and the Arts, 1943-1965*. Philadelphia, 1983.

Lawrence, Vera Brodsky, *Strong on Music*. New York, 1987.

Levine, Faye, *The Culture Barons*. New York, 1976

Lewis, R.W.B., *The American Adam*. Chicago, 1955.

Munro McClosky, *Our National Attic*. New York, 1968.

Madden, David, *Proletarian Writers of the Thirties*. Carbondale, Ill., 1967.

Mangione, Jere, *The Dream and the Deal: The Federal Writers' Project, 1935-1943*. New York, 1972.

Marquis, Alice Goldfarb, *Art Lessons: Learning from the Rise and Fall of Public Arts Funding. New York, 1995*

Mathews, Jane DeHart, *The Federal Theatre, 1935-39: Plays, Relief, and Politics*. Princeton, 1967.

Matthiessen, F.O., *The American Renaissance*. New York, 1941.

McDonald, William F., *Federal Relief Administration and the Arts*. Columbus, Ohio, 1968.

McKinzie, Richard D., *The New Deal for Artists*. Princeton, 1973.

McMullen, Roy, *Art, Affluence and Alienation: The Fine Arts Today*. New York, 1968.

Miller, Lillian, *Patrons and Patronage, The Encouragement of the Fine Arts in the United States, 1790-1860*. Chicago, 1966.

Miller, Perry, *The Transcendentalists*, Boston, 1953.

Mulcahy, K. and C.R. Swain, *Public Policy and the Arts*, Boulder, 1982.

Netzer, Dick, *The Subsidized Muse: Public Support for the Arts in the United States.* Cambridge, 1978.

Nye, Russell, *The Cultural Life of the New Nation, 1776-1830.* New York, 1960.

O'Connor, Francis V., *Federal Support for the Visual Arts: The New Deal and Now.* Greenwich, Conn., 1969.

Oehser, Paul Henry, *The Smithsonian Institution.* New York, 1970.

Overmyer, Grace, *Government and the Arts.* New York, 1939.

Persons, Stowe, *The Decline of American Civility.* New York, 1973.

Purcell, Ralph, *Government and Art: A Study of the American Experience.* Washington, D.C., 1956.

Reval, Elisabeth, *Alexandre Vattemare trait d'Union Entre Deux Mondes.* Montreal, 1975.

Richardson, Edgar, *Painting in America.* New York, 1956.

_____, *Washington Allston, A Study of the Romantic Artist in America.* Chicago, 1948.

Rideout, Walter, *The Radical Novel in the United States, 1900-1954.* Cambridge, Mass., 1956.

Schuyler, David, *The New Urban Landscape.* Baltimore, 1986.

Sclar, Charlotte, *The Smithsonian.* Jefferson, NC, 1985.

Sizer, Theodore (ed.), *The Autobiography of Colonel John Trumbull, Patriot-Artist, 1756-1843.* New Haven, 1943.

Smith, Henry Nash, *Virgin Land.* Cambridge, 1950.

Spencer, Benjamin T., *The Quest for Nationality.* Syracuse, 1957.

Swados, Harvey, ed., *The American Writer and the Great Depression.* Indianapolis, Ind., 1966.

Toffler, Alvin, *The Culture Consumers: A Study of Art and Affluence in America.* Baltimore, 1965.

Tomsich, John, *A Genteel Endeavor.* Stanford, 1971.

Weeter, Dixon, *The Saga of American Society.* New York, 1937.

Wertenbaker, T.J., *The Old South; The Founding of American Civilization.* New York, 1942.

Willey, Basil, *The Eighteenth Century Background.* London, 1949.

Wright, Louis B. *Culture on the Moving Frontier.* Bloomington, Ind., 1955.

Wyeth, S.D., *The Federal City.* Washington, 1865.

Young, James S., *The Washington Community 1800-1828.* New York, 1966.

Index